Life of Dante

Life of Dante

Giovanni Boccaccio

Translated by J.G. Nichols

ET REMOTISSIMA PROPE

100 PAGES

100 PAGES
Published by Hesperus Press Limited
4 Rickett Street, London SW6 1RU
www.hesperuspress.com

First published by Hesperus Press Limited, 2002

English language translation and Introduction © J.G. Nichols, 2002
Foreword © A.N. Wilson, 2002

Designed and typeset by Fraser Muggeridge
Printed in the United Arab Emirates by Oriental Press

ISBN: 1-84391-006-3

CONTENTS

FOREWORD

The life of Italy's greatest poet (Dante Alighieri, 1265–1321) is contained in his *Divina Commedia*, the extraordinary three-tiered journey which began in a dark wood 'nel mezzo del cammin di nostra vita' [in the middle of our life's journey] and ended with the beatific vision of God himself. Dante's marvellous poem is, for most non-Italians, the great unread masterpiece. They are deterred from starting it because they do not know where to take hold of it. Picking up an edition of the *Inferno*, the first of the volumes, they find, even in a translation, endless allusions in the notes to classical mythology, to medieval philosophy and theology, and to the impenetrable feuds and battles between rival groups of thirteenth-century Italians. While struggling to hold in their heads the answer to the question: 'Was Dante a Guelph or a Ghibelline, a Black or a White?', they have forgotten who the Guelphs and Ghibellines were in the first place.

In a sense, our generation is over-educated. We feel that in order to read something we ought to be able to pass an exam in it. We are frightened of Shakespeare without the notes. If we go to the opera we want to prepare ourselves first by obsessive listening to a recording, or reading of the score.

Earlier generations plunged in, and took these great works for what they were. The *Commedia* is many things, but among them it is an autobiography. Dante is centre stage all the time, dramatising and melodramatising his situation. Thus, mingled with the story of mankind's fall, purgation and redemption, is the story of how one man's attempts at a political career in Florence came unstuck when the party whom he supported fell from power and he was exiled from his beloved city-state. His wandering and homesickness become an emblem of the human exile from paradise. In the circles of hell and purgatory, as well as meeting the great sinners of mythology and history, he constantly encounters those from his own life, his teachers, his colleagues, his enemies. In heaven itself he meets his ancestor Cacciaguida (1091–1147) who proudly traces his pedigree back to the Romans. 'From Cacciaguida to Dante', says Barbara Reynolds in her commentary, 'flows not only the blood of illustrious forbears but also the past events of Florence, the history of Christendom, the inheritance of sin and of redemption, the burden and the glory of the Cross.' Cacciaguida remembers a time when Florence was a sturdy Republican commune in which the aristocratic ideals of valour and honesty prevailed. The decline of Florence, real in Dante's eyes, is also seen as an allegory of the decline of the world itself into sin and corruption. Cacciaguida died serving in the Second Crusade under the Emperor Conrad III. He is a warrior for Christ.

Everything in Dante's autobiography becomes allegorised and generalised. The one biographical detail which everyone knows about him is that when he was nine years old he met a little girl called Bice (or Beatrice), the daughter of a banker called Folco Portinari. His spiritual obsession with her became intense, especially when, in her twenty-fourth year, she died. The entire spiritual journey of the *Commedia* is seen, in part, as an attempt to regain the vision of this lost 'love' – which is not primarily a sexual love, but the deepest passion of his life. (One of his later mistresses, known only to us as the 'noble' or 'kind lady', 'la donna gentile', with whom he clearly had a real affair, is allegorised in his other works as Philosophy distracting him from the memory of the Bringer of Blessings [Beatrice] who allegorically represents Theology.)

All this should be enough to make clear that Dante's life,

(or perhaps one should put inverted commas around that and say 'Dante's Life') was the central framework of his poetry and his art.

Giovanni Boccaccio (1313–75) is best known to us perhaps as the author of the *Decameron*, that rich compilation of stories, mainly love-stories, many of them ribald, which inspired Chaucer's *Canterbury Tales*. (His prose romance, *Filostrato*, was translated and transformed by Chaucer into *Troilus and Criseyde*). Boccaccio was Dante's first biographer, and in his lectures on Dante's life and work, delivered in Florence after Dante died, he was also the first great interpreter of his work.

Boccaccio's *Life of Dante* is a good introduction to the modern reader; an even better one for readers who might consider themselves post-modern. The reason I say this is that Boccaccio is not attempting in this book to write a realistic life of Dante. The number of facts which are indisputable about Dante is very few. Did Dante really, as he claimed, go to Paris to study theology? Was he really a novice in the Franciscan order? We can not disentangle these claims of his from the emblematic uses he makes of them in his poetry. Because Boccaccio is himself a poet, he enters into Dante's self-vision and world-vision with peculiar aplomb. He is not searching, as a modern biographer might do, for the 'real Dante' among the desk-drawers of discontented wives, abandoned mistresses or neglected children. He searches instead in the most obvious place, in Dante's work.

True, to Boccaccio we also owe some of the crucial chatty information which we want to know about any of the great men and women of the past. Boccaccio tells us for example what Dante looked like: 'He was always dressed in good clothes of a fashion appropriate to his years. His face was long, his nose aquiline, his eyes rather big, his jaw large, and his lower lip protruded beyond the upper. His complexion was dark, his hair and beard thick, black and curly, and his expression was melancholy and thoughtful.'

As we should expect from the poet who meditated more than any other on the tragi-farce of unhappy marriage, Boccaccio noted the fact that when Dante went into exile, he did not take his wife with him, and recognises that Dante's wife seems to have been the only woman in his life who did not merit so much as an ode, let alone a beatific vision. 'Who does not know that everything which is bought is tried by the purchaser before he buys it, except a wife?' says Boccaccio, momentarily making Dante and his lady seem like the more ridiculously ill-matched pairs in the *Decameron*.

The bulk of Boccaccio's *Life* however is devoted to exposing the nature of Dante the poet. Although it relates to a man who lived and suffered and died, this book is not a biography in the modern sense of the word. It is as much a work of the imagination as the *Decameron* or the *Divine Comedy*. It begins with the prophetic dream of Dante's mother: that she gave birth to a boy who ate of the berries which fell from a laurel tree, that he was transformed into a shepherd who took the laurel leaves, and then into a flamboyant peacock. The story ends with Boccaccio's exposition of this entirely 'unrealistic' portrait. It is a reminder that what interests us primarily about a great artist is not the gossipy detail of his private life but the spiritual essence of his work. Boccaccio's *Life of Dante* is not merely the first of thousands of books written about Dante; it is in more than one sense primary, for it retains and explains Dante's own preoccupation with his vision, while helping us to understand that vision more clearly.

– A.N. Wilson, 2002

INTRODUCTION

Boccaccio's *Life of Dante* may well be considered the first modern literary biography. It is certainly the first biography of Dante, and the source of many of the facts upon which later biographers have drawn. And its modernity is often surprising. Boccaccio gives us those personal details about his subject which all biographers of today, and their readers, delight in. He tells us what Dante looked like and how he dressed, and describes some of his most characteristic traits. He gives us more detail on Dante's first meeting with Beatrice than does Dante himself in his *Vita nuova* (*New Life*), and also speculates on some of the possible psychological causes of the effect that this meeting had on Dante. He even tells us how Dante's wife managed to survive financially during his exile. This is hardly as important to us now as it must have been to her then, but it is a telling detail which helps to fill in the background and convince us of the writer's intimate knowledge. Again, the intricacies of Florentine politics in Dante's day are difficult for even the interested reader to follow, but Boccaccio outlines them clearly, mainly in order to contrast Dante's probity with the evil rampant in his native city and hence bring out further facets of Dante's character. Moreover, although Boccaccio's avowed purpose in writing is to praise Florence's greatest son – one common title used for this work in Italian is *Trattatello in laude di Dante* (A short essay in praise of Dante) – he does tell us of Dante's faults, admittedly without revelling in them as a modern biographer would. We do feel that Boccaccio would have appreciated the force, without necessarily approving the style, of an anecdote told later in the same century by Franco Sacchetti. This describes an incident said to have occurred while Dante was still living in Florence and when he was passing through the district of Porta di San Piero, his home area:

'...a blacksmith, while he beat away on his anvil, was singing Dante's poem [the *Divine Comedy*] in the same way as people sing popular ballads, mixing the lines up, leaving bits out, and adding bits. And so Dante felt deeply insulted. He didn't say anything, but he went up to the smithy where all the blacksmith's tools were. Then he got hold of the hammer and threw it into the street, got the pincers and threw them into the street, and got the scales and threw them into the street. And in this manner he threw many of the tools away.

The blacksmith, turning towards him savagely, said, "What the devil are you doing? Are you crazy?"

Dante said, "I might ask what you're doing."

"I am doing my job," said the blacksmith. "And you're damaging my tools, throwing them into the street."

Dante said, "If you don't want me to spoil your things, then don't spoil mine."

The blacksmith said, "But what am I spoiling of yours?"

Dante said, "You're singing my poem, and you're not singing it as I wrote it. This is the only job I have, and you're spoiling it for me."

The blacksmith, really angry, but not knowing how to reply, gathered up his things and went back to his work. And afterwards, when he felt like singing, he sang of Tristan and Lancelot, and left Dante's poem alone...' (From *Il trecentonovelle.*)

Giovanni Boccaccio was exceptionally well qualified to write Dante's biography. He was a Florentine, and he was acquainted with Dante's daughter Beatrice, with Dante's nephew, with at least two of Dante's close friends, and also with a near relative of Dante's great love, Beatrice Portinari. Although the two never met – Dante was forty-eight when Boccaccio was born, and he had by then been living in exile for thirteen years – their intellectual as well as their physical backgrounds were very similar. Consequently when Boccaccio writes of the history of their native city, and of its politics and its poetry, and of the Italian language and its history, he not only knows what he is writing about but is deeply involved in it all. His discussions of literary matters – the origin of poetry, the relation of poetry to theology, and the reasons for crowning poets with laurel – do present difficulties to a modern reader, simply because we view these matters from a twenty-first century standpoint. But it is always healthy for us to be so disturbed in our preconceptions. Moreover, Boccaccio starts from the same place, spiritually as well as physically, as Dante, and so he has no difficulty in presenting him in the context of his time. One further and supreme qualification was that Boccaccio was a literary genius. His most famous work is of course the *Decameron*, whose quality is well exemplified by that story which sparkles with the wit and presence of mind of Dante's best friend, Guido Cavalcanti (see page 81). This literary ability and persuasiveness are amply demonstrated in his life of Dante. He manages both to persuade us of his reliability and reveal his conscious employment of literary cunning when he says of Dante: '…if I am silent about anything that was not praiseworthy in him, I shall destroy the faith of the reader in the praiseworthy virtues which I have already pointed out.' Again, there is his remark at the end of his description of the miseries of marriage: 'Of course I do not affirm that these things fell to Dante's lot, for I do not know.'

This shows an honesty we should always require of biographers, and it is also very persuasive in bringing the reader onto the biographer's side. Dante, Petrarch, and Boccaccio are the founding fathers of Italian literature, and we are extremely fortunate to have a biography of the greatest of these by one of the other two. What would we in England not give for, say, such a detailed and studied biography of Shakespeare by Ben Jonson, or one of Chaucer if he had had a contemporary fit to write it? (Indeed, Ben Jonson's scattered comments on his friend show what we are missing.)

This biography is not faultless, and the section most open to criticism is the long attack on marriage in the third chapter. We can defend it to some extent. Boccaccio does say that he means simply that marriage is not a suitable state for all, and certainly not for philosophers (by which he means literary men or scholars). We may therefore consider he is seeing it as a hindrance to intellectual and creative endeavour, a fourteenth-century version of 'the pram in the hall'. But Boccaccio really goes far beyond this and, whatever we may think of his opinions, they are artistically out of place here, particularly since he admits he has no knowledge that Dante suffered any of the woes he mentions. The earlier list of Dante's troubles – 'Dante was the prey of the fierce and unendurable passion of love, and he had a wife, and public and private responsibilities, and he suffered exile and poverty' – can be seen as comic, and an example of knee-jerk misogyny and the traditional tendency 'to speke of wo that is in mariage' (Chaucer, *The Wife of Bath's Prologue*). In the end, however, this lengthy diatribe reveals too much about Boccaccio and quite possibly nothing about Dante.

There are other passages which may well startle us, but these, I think, ought to startle us out of any complacency we may have over our way of seeing things. There is the dream that Dante's mother had when she was pregnant with him. This is certainly very detailed and highly coloured. But then dreams often are. And that a mother should dream that her son will be someone special is not, I think, uncommon. The only extraordinary thing here is that she was right. Boccaccio's allegorical explanation of the dream, which is ingenious and detailed even though he assures us it is 'a very superficial explanation', may strike us as odd, but is really no odder than our own automatic love, post-Freud, of interpreting our dreams psychologically. The account of the finding of the lost and last thirteen cantos of the *Paradiso* by Dante's son Iacopo, which again concerns a dream, has nothing unlikely in it. Was Iacopo really unaware of the hole in the wall? Or had he once known it, forgotten it, and then remembered it again in a dream? In asking those questions I am interpreting psychologically what Boccaccio sees as providential, and the two interpretations need not exclude each other. It is interesting that Barbara Reynolds who, after the death of Dorothy L. Sayers, completed her fine translation of the *Divine Comedy*, mentions that the work she was left with did not, except for a few fragments, proceed beyond the twentieth canto of the *Paradiso*, leaving the same thirteen cantos still to be provided. Modestly she calls this 'a strange coincidence', but the fact that she mentions it at all does remind us that we can never be sure what is merely coincidental and what is providential.

Boccaccio was an early enthusiast for Dante's works, at a time when Dante's superiority to his forerunners and contemporaries was by no means so obvious as it is now, and his superiority to all his successors could only have been guessed at. In his native city especially, his writings were often the object of great suspicion from the earliest days. And there was a cardinal in Bologna who had *De monarchia* burned. He also wanted to dig up Dante's bones and add them to the fire, and was with difficulty persuaded that this was not really necessary. More than two hundred years after that, a Florentine edition of the *New Life* was only licensed to be printed in a bowdlerised form. Great credit is due to Boccaccio for his recognition of the unique importance of Dante and also for providing us with a book which is not only a great help to an appreciation of the master but a fine literary work in its own right.

– *J.G. Nichols, 2002*

ACKNOWLEDGEMENTS

This translation of *Life of Dante* is taken from the edition of Giovanni Boccaccio's *Trattatello in laude di Dante,* edited by Luigi Sasso (Garzanti, Milan, 1995). The sonnet, 'Dante Speaks', is taken from the anthology, *Rime di M. Cino da Pistoia e d'altri del Secolo XIV*, edited by Giosuè Carducci (Istituto Editoriale Italiano, Milan, no date).

Life of Dante

Dante Speaks

My name is Dante, and my mind was full
Of artistry and understanding which
Brought natural eloquence to such a pitch
Nature still sees it as a miracle.

I crossed the realms, in my deep fantasy,
Of the unhappy and the happy dead,
And made my volume worthy to be read
In a worldly or otherworldly way.

The famed City of Florence was my mother,
Or wicked stepmother to her true child,
The fault being evil tongues that know no honour.

Ravenna took me when I was exiled,
And has my body, but my soul the Father
Preserves where envy never has prevailed.

– Giovanni Boccaccio

CHAPTER ONE

Proem

Solon, whose breast was said to be a human temple of divine wisdom, and whose sacred laws are to the men of today an illustrious witness to the justice of the ancients, was, according to some, in the habit of declaring that every republic walks and stands, like ourselves, on two feet. In his mature wisdom he affirmed that the right foot consists of not letting any crime that has been committed remain unpunished, and the left of rewarding every good deed. He added that whenever either of these two things was neglected, whether by corruption or by carelessness, or was not well seen to, then the republic must without doubt be lame. And if, by some great misfortune, it sinned on both counts, then it was almost inevitable that it could not stand at all.

Struck by this praiseworthy and obviously sound maxim, many ancient and famous peoples honoured their worthy men, sometimes by deifying them, sometimes by marble statues, often by distinguished funerals and triumphal arches and laurel crowns, according to their merits. The punishments inflicted on the guilty, on the other hand, I do not care to recount. It was by virtue of such honours and penalties that Assyria, Macedonia, Greece, and finally the Roman Republic grew until their deeds reached to the ends of the earth and their fame touched the stars. Their successors, especially my fellow-citizens of Florence, have not only failed to follow in the footsteps of such high exemplars, but have so far wandered from them that ambition now receives all the rewards due to virtue. Therefore I, and anyone else who looks at the matter rationally, can see, and not without the greatest affliction of heart, evil and perverse men elevated to high places and supreme offices and rewarded, and good men exiled, cast down, and humbled. Let those who steer our ship of state consider what end the justice of God may reserve for those practices, since we common people are borne along by the tide, and by Fortune's blast, but are not sharers in their guilt. Although what has been said above may be confirmed by innumerable clear instances of ingratitude to the good and criminal leniency to the bad, one instance alone will suffice for me at least to reveal our own faults and come to my main point. And this instance will not be an unimportant one, for I refer to the exile of the illustrious Dante Alighieri, born of an old citizen family – not of low parentage. What rewards he deserved for his worth, his learning, and his good service are amply apparent, and will be shown by his actions, as we shall see. If such deeds had been done in a just republic, there is no doubt that they would have won him the highest rewards.

Oh, what a horrible thought, infamous deed, wretched example, manifest sign of ruin to come! In place of reward, he suffered an unjust and hasty sentence, perpetual banishment, the alienation of his family estate, and, if such a thing could have been accomplished, the staining of his glorious fame by false accusations. To this the fresh traces of his wanderings, his bones buried in another country, his children scattered in others' houses, still in part bear witness. If all the other iniquities of Florence could be concealed from the all-seeing eyes of God, would not this alone suffice to draw down upon it His wrath? Yes, indeed! Of those who, on the other hand, have been exalted, I judge that it is better to remain silent.

Looking well, then, at the facts, we see that today's world has not only left the path of the early world, on which I touched above, but has turned its feet in the opposite direction. So it is clear enough that if we, and others who live as we do, contrary to Solon's maxim, still stand on our feet without falling, there can be no other reason than that through long usage the nature of things has changed, as we often see happen. Or perhaps it is a special miracle, by which God, on account of some merit in one of our ancestors, sustains us, contrary to all human expectation. Or perhaps it is His patience, awaiting our repentance. And if our repentance does not eventually follow, let no one doubt that His anger, which moves with slow pace towards vengeance, reserves for us a punishment so much more grievous that it will compensate for its tardiness.

But as we should not only flee evil deeds, though they seem to go unpunished, but also by right action try to correct them, I, recognising that I am of the same city as Dante Alighieri (though I am but a small part and he a very great part of it, if his merits, his nobility, and his worth be considered), feel that, like every other citizen, I am personally obliged to honour him. Although I am not sufficient for so great a task, nevertheless, what the city ought to have done for him in a magnificent fashion, but has not done, I will endeavour to do, according to my own poor ability. This will not be with a statue or noble burial, the custom of which has now perished among us (nor would my power suffice), but by my writing, which is a humble instrument for so great an undertaking. This I can and will do, so that foreign nations will not be able to say that, both as a body and individually, his native land has been ungrateful to so great a poet. And I shall describe (in a humble and contemporary style, because my talent does not allow me to go higher, and in our own Florentine idiom, that it may be in keeping with the language he used in most of his works) those things about which he preserved a modest silence. By this, I mean the nobility of his origin, his life, his

7

studies, and his habits. Then I shall sum up the works by which he has made himself so very illustrious among generations yet to come. My words may obscure him as much as throw light on him, but this is by no means my intention. I shall always be glad in this and other matters to be corrected by those wiser than I, when I have spoken in error. So that this may not happen, I humbly pray Him who, as we know, drew Dante up such a long ascent to see Him, that He will now aid me, and guide my intellect and my feeble hand.

CHAPTER TWO

Dante's birth and education

Florence, as was the case with the most noble of the other Italian cities, took her beginning from the Romans, as the ancient historians tell us and as the common opinion of the people now has it. In the course of time she grew larger, became full of people and of illustrious citizens, and began to appear to her neighbours as not merely a city but a powerful one. Whether the ultimate cause of the change was adverse fortune, or the ill will of heaven, or the deserts of her citizens, is uncertain. However, it is clear that, not many centuries later, Attila, the cruel king of the Vandals and the general devastator of nearly all Italy, killed and dispersed all, or the greater part of, those citizens who were famous for noble blood or for other reasons, and reduced Florence itself to ashes and ruins. So it remained, we believe, for more than three hundred years. At the end of that time the imperial power of Rome was transferred, with good reason, from Greece to Gaul, and Charlemagne, the most merciful King of France, was raised to the imperial throne. After his many labours, he was moved, I believe, by the divine spirit, to turn his imperial mind to the rebuilding of this desolate city. Although he limited its size by a small circuit of walls, he had it rebuilt, so far as he could, after the likeness of Rome, and settled it with those who had been its first founders, collecting inside the walls the few remnants that could be found of the descendants of the ancient exiles.

Among these new inhabitants – perhaps he who super-intended the rebuilding, or assigned the houses and streets, or gave to this new people the necessary laws – there came from

Rome, so the story runs, a noble youth of the family of the Frangipani, called by everyone Eliseo. It so happened that, after he had accomplished his principal purpose, he became a permanent resident of the city. He was attracted either by love for the city which he had so recently helped to reorganise, or by the pleasant site, to which he may have seen that heaven must be favourable in future, or by some other cause. When he died he left a large and worthy family of sons and descendants who, abandoning the ancient surname of their ancestors, took the name of him who had founded their family, and all called themselves the Elisei. As time went on and son succeeded father, there was born and lived in this family a brave knight, remarkable for both his deeds and his wisdom, whose name was Cacciaguida. To him, in his youth, his elders gave for his bride a maiden born of the Aldighieri family of Ferrara, esteemed for her beauty and character as well as for her noble blood, with whom he lived for many years, and by whom he had many children. Although she was not unduly concerned with the names of her other children, she chose to revive for one the name of her ancestors, as women like to do, naming him Aldighieri, although the word afterwards, dropping the letter *d*, became Alighieri. The worth of this man brought it about that all who descended from him forsook the surname of Elisei, and instead called themselves Alighieri – a practice which has lasted to our time. From him descended many children, and grandchildren, and great-grandchildren, and, in the reign of the Emperor Frederick II, one whose name was Alighieri, and who was destined to become illustrious through his son rather than by his own merit. His wife, when she was with child and not far from the time of giving birth, saw in a dream what the fruit of her womb would be. Although this dream was not then understood by her or by anyone else, it is now clear to all from what followed.

It seemed to the noble lady in her dream that she was under a lofty laurel tree in a green meadow, near a clear spring, and here she felt herself give birth to a son, who, in a brief space of time, feeding only upon the berries which fell from the laurel tree, and drinking the waters of the clear spring, seemed to her to become a shepherd, and to strive with all his might to lay hold of the leaves of the laurel tree whose fruit had fed him. And in striving for this, he seemed to her to fall, and on rising, to have become no longer a man but a peacock. At this she was so astonished that she awoke, and soon the time came for her labour, and she gave birth to a son, to whom she and his father agreed to give the name of Dante. This was appropriate because, as we shall see later, the result fitted the name excellently.[1] This was that Dante of whom I write. This was that Dante who was granted to our age by the special grace of God. This was that Dante who was destined to be the first to open the way for the return to Italy of the banished Muses. By him the glory of the Florentine idiom was made manifest. By him all the beauties of our common speech were set to a fitting rhythm. By him dead poetry may properly be said to have been revived. These things, when they are carefully considered, show that he could rightly have had no other name but Dante.

This glory of the Italian race was born in our city when the imperial throne was vacant through the death of Frederick II, whom I have already mentioned, in the year of the saving Incarnation of the King of the Universe 1265, while Pope Urban the Fourth sat in the chair of St Peter. He was born into a family on whom Fortune smiled – I say 'smiled' according to the quality of the world at that time. But, however that may have been, ignoring his infancy, in which appeared many signs of the future glory of his intellect, I say that from the beginning of his boyhood, when he had learned the first elements of his letters, he did not give himself up, after the fashion of the young nobles of today, to boyish frivolity and sloth, lounging in his mother's lap. He gave up his entire boyhood, in his own city, to the continued study of the liberal arts, in which he became admirably expert.

And as his mind and intelligence increased with years, he did not devote himself to lucrative studies as most people now do, but, with a praiseworthy desire for eternal fame, and, despising transitory riches, he gave himself up completely to his wish to gain full knowledge of the fictions of the poets and of the critical analysis of them. In this study he became thoroughly familiar with Virgil, Horace, Ovid, Statius, and every other famous poet. He not only took delight in knowing them, but he strove to imitate them in lofty song, as is shown in the works of which we shall speak in their proper time. And seeing that the works of the poets are not vain and simple fables or marvels, as the foolish multitude thinks, but that within them are concealed the sweet fruits of historical and philosophical truth (for which reason the intent of the poets cannot be wholly understood without a knowledge of history and moral and natural philosophy), he made a sensible division of his time, and strove to learn history by himself and philosophy under various masters, and not without long study and toil. And seized by the sweetness of knowing the truth about heavenly things, and finding nothing else in life dearer than this, he put all other earthly cares completely aside, and devoted himself entirely to this quest. And in order that he might leave no part of philosophy uninvestigated, his acute mind explored the most profound depths of theology. And the result was not far distant from the intention. With no regard for heat or cold, vigils or fasts, or any other bodily discomfort, by assiduous study he came to know whatever the human intellect can know here of the Divine Essence and of the angels. And as at various stages of his life he studied various branches of knowledge, so he prosecuted his various studies under various masters.

The first elements, as I have said, he found in his native city. From here, as to a place richer in such food, he went to Bologna. By the time he was approaching old age, he went to Paris where he showed the height of his genius in many disputations, with such glory to himself that those who heard him still wonder as they tell the tale. As a result of studies of this sort, he won, not unjustly, the very highest titles. During his life he was hailed by some as 'poet', by others, 'philosopher', and by many, 'theologian'. But since victory is the more glorious to the victor as the strength of the vanquished is greater, I judge it to be appropriate first to show on what a surging and tempestuous sea, tossed now here, now there, vanquishing alike the waves and the contrary winds, he came to the safe harbour of those illustrious titles.

CHAPTER THREE

Dante's love for Beatrice and his marriage

Studies generally require solitude, freedom from care, and tranquillity of mind, and this is especially true for speculative studies, such as those to which Dante, as has been shown, gave himself up completely. But in place of this freedom and quiet, almost from the beginning of his life to the day of his death, Dante was the prey of the fierce and unendurable passion of love, and he had a wife, and public and private responsibilities, and he suffered exile and poverty. Leaving aside other more particular cares which these necessarily bring with them, I think it right to mention these burdens one by one, so that their weight may be more evident.

In the season when the sweetness of heaven reclothes the earth with its adornments, and makes it smile with various kinds of flowers among the green leaves, it was the custom in our city for men and women to hold festivals, all in their own districts and with their own friends. So it happened that Folco Portinari, a man much honoured among his fellow-citizens at that time, gathered his neighbours together in his own house for a feast on the first day of May. Among these was the aforementioned Alighieri, who was followed by Dante (who had not yet finished his ninth year), just as small boys will follow their fathers, especially to places of festival. Here, mingling with others of his own age (for there were many such in the house of his host, both boys and girls), when the first tables had been served, he gave himself up to playing like a child with the others, so far as his tender years permitted. There was among the crowd of children a little daughter of Folco Portinari, whose name was Bice (although he always called her by her full name, Beatrice), who was perhaps eight years old, very comely for her age, and very gentle and pleasing in her actions, with ways and words more serious and modest than her youth required. Besides this, her features were very delicate and well formed, and so full of beauty and modest grace that she was declared by many to be like a little angel. She then, such as I paint her and perhaps even more beautiful, appeared at this feast to the eyes of our Dante, not, I believe, for the first time, but for the first time with power to enamour him. And although a mere boy, he received her beautiful image into his heart with such affection that from that day forward it never departed while he lived. What this image was like, no one knows. But (whether it was the likeness of their temperaments or habits, or some special influence of heaven, or, as we know occurs at feasts, the sweetness of the music, the common joy, the delicacy of the meats and wines, that can make the hearts of mature men – much more of young people – more open to be caught by whatever pleases them) it certainly happened that Dante, at this tender age, became a most fervent slave of love. Leaving aside any discussion of childish details, I declare that with age the flames of his love increased, so that nothing else was pleasure or repose or comfort to him except seeing her. So, neglecting everything else, he would go most assiduously where he believed that he could see her, as if from her face and eyes he would obtain his every happiness and complete consolation.

Oh, senseless judgement of lovers! Who else but they would think to make the fire less by adding fuel to it? What deep thoughts he had, what sighs he breathed, what tears he shed, and what other grievous passions he suffered in later life, he himself in part shows us in his work, *New Life*, and therefore I do not care to go into them in more detail. There is only one thing that I must mention. As he himself writes, and as others to whom his desire was known report, his love was most virtuous, and there never appeared, by look or word or sign, any wanton appetite either in the lover or in her whom he loved. This is no small marvel in today's world, from which all virtuous pleasure has so fled, and which is so accustomed to having whatever pleases it available to its lust, even before it has decided to love, that it has become a miracle, inasmuch as it is the rarest of things, that anyone could love in any other way. If so great and so lasting love could keep him from food, sleep, and all manner of rest, what power must we think it had as an adversary of his sacred studies and his genius! No small power, certainly, although many will have it that love incited his genius, and they prove this by his graceful rhymes in the Florentine idiom, which were made by him to praise his beloved lady and to express his ardours and his amorous reflections. However, to agree with this I would have to concede that ornate discourse is the principal part of every branch of knowledge, which is not true.

As everyone can readily understand, there is nothing stable in this world, and if there is one thing that changes easily, it is our life. A little too much cold or heat, leaving aside innumerable tiny accidents and possibilities, takes us without difficulty from existence to non-existence. No gentility, riches, youth, or any other mundane dignity is ever exempt from this. The weight of this common law Dante had to learn by another's death before his own. The beautiful Beatrice was nearly at the end of her twenty-fourth year when, as pleased Him who is all-powerful, she left the anguish of this world and departed to the glory which her own merits had prepared for her. At her departure Dante was left in such sorrow, grief, and tears that many of those nearest him, both relatives and friends, believed there could be no other conclusion but his death. This they thought must come quickly, seeing that he would listen to no comfort or consolation offered him. The days were like the nights, and the nights like the days. No hour of either passed without cries and sighs and many tears. His eyes seemed two copious fountains of flowing water, so that most marvelled where he acquired enough moisture to supply his weeping. But, just as we see that passions by long custom become easy to bear, and similarly that in time all things diminish and perish, it happened that Dante, in the course of several months, came to remember without tears that Beatrice was dead. With better judgement, as sorrow began to give way to reason, he came to recognise that neither weeping nor sighs nor anything else could restore his lost lady to him. Therefore, with more patience, he set himself to endure the loss of her presence, and not long after his tears were stopped his sighs, which were even then near their end, began in great measure to depart and not return.

By his weeping, by the pain in his heart, and by taking no care of himself, he had taken on the appearance of a wild thing. He was lean, unshaven, and almost completely transformed from what he had been before. His appearance aroused pity, not only in his friends, but in everyone who saw him, although while this tearful life of his lasted, he let himself be seen by few others than his friends. Their compassion and their fear of the worst made his relatives attentive to his comfort, and when they saw his tears were ceasing to flow and realised that his heavy sighs were ceasing to trouble his heart, they began once more to urge on the disconsolate lover that consolation which had so long been in vain. And he, who up to that time had obstinately closed his ears to all consolation, now began not only to open them somewhat, but to listen willingly to what was said for his comfort. Seeing this, his relatives, so that they might not only take him out of his grief, but bring him back to joy again, discussed the possibility of finding him a wife. As his lost lady had been the occasion of grief, so one newly acquired might be the cause of gladness. They found a young girl who was suitable for his station in life, and, with arguments that appeared to them most convincing, they revealed their intention to him. And, without going into details, after long and almost uninterrupted discussions, their arguments were effective and he was married.

Oh blind minds, darkened intellects, and vain reasoning of so many mortals! How contrary to your expectation, and often with good reason, is the outcome in so many matters! Who would ever, because of the excessive heat, take someone away from the sweet air of Italy to the burning sands of Libya for refreshment? Or who, to warm someone, would ever take him from the Isle of Cyprus to the eternal shadows of the Rhodopean Mountains? What physician would endeavour to expel an acute fever with fire, or drive away the chill from the marrow of one's bones with ice or snow? Certainly no one would, except those who think that a bride will lessen the tribulations of love. Those who think to do this do not understand the nature of love, or how it adds every other passion to itself. In vain is aid or counsel pitted against its force if it has once taken firm root in the heart of one who has loved for a long time. Just as at first the slightest resistance is helpful, so in the course of time the strongest tends to be harmful. But it is time to return to our subject, and for the present to leave aside those things which may make one forget the troubles of love.

What then has he achieved who, to relieve me of one annoying thought, brings me others a thousand times greater and more annoying? Certainly nothing but, by adding to my ills, made me desire to return to those from which he has drawn me. This is something which we often see happen to people who, to escape or be drawn from trouble, blindly marry or are married by others. They do not perceive that, by escaping from one set of complications, they have entered into a thousand others, until experience proves it to them when they can no longer change their minds and go back. His relatives and friends gave Dante a wife in order that his tears for Beatrice might cease. But I do not know whether, although his tears passed away (or rather, perhaps, had already passed away), the flame of love passed away for that reason. Indeed, I do not believe it, but, even if that flame had been extinguished, new and greater troubles were now able to come upon him.

Accustomed to devote himself by night to his sacred studies, he was wont to converse as often as he pleased with emperors, kings, and all other exalted princes of the earth, dispute with philosophers, and find pleasure with the most delightful poets, mitigating his own sorrows by listening to theirs. But now he could be with them only so long as it pleased his bride, and whenever she wished to withdraw him from such high company, he was obliged to spend his time listening to womanish conversation which, if he wanted to avoid further annoyance, he had, against his will, not only to agree to but to praise. He was accustomed, whenever the vulgar crowd wearied him, to withdraw into some solitary place, and there to speculate what spirit moves the heavens, whence comes the life of all creatures on earth, and what are the causes of things, or brood over strange ideas, or compose verses whose fame should after his death make him live to posterity. But now he was not only deprived of all this pleasant contemplation at the whim of his bride, but he had to keep company with those who are ill-suited to such things. He was accustomed to laugh, to weep, to sing, or to sigh freely, as sweet or bitter passions moved him. Now, however, he either did not dare to do so, or he had to give account to his wife, not only of important things but even of the slightest sigh, showing its cause, where it came from, and where it went. This was because she believed his joy was occasioned by love for someone else, his sadness by hate for her.

Oh, what an inordinate weariness it is, having to live, to converse, and finally grow old and die with such a suspicious creature! I will not even mention the new and weighty troubles which must be borne by those unaccustomed to them, especially in our city: the provision of clothing, ornaments, and rooms full of superfluous luxuries which women make themselves believe are necessary for living properly; the provision of menservants and womenservants, and nurses, and chambermaids; the provision of dinners, and gifts, and the presents which must be given to brides' relatives, whom husbands want their wives to think they love; and in addition to this all the things previously unknown to free men. And what of those things that are impossible to avoid? Who doubts that people at large judge the beauty of one's wife? If she be reputed fair, who doubts that she will at once have many admirers who will incessantly attack her unstable heart with their looks, their rank, their wonderful flattery, their gifts, or their pleasing manners? And that which many desire is very hard to protect. And it is only necessary for a woman's chastity to be overcome once to make her forever infamous and her husband forever unhappy. What if, by her husband's misfortune, she be ugly? Since we can clearly see that men often enough and all too quickly tire even of the most beautiful, what can we think of such women but that their husbands will hate not only them but every place in which they are likely to be found by those who must have them always with them? This is why women become angry – and no wild beast is so fierce as an angry woman. A man's life cannot be safe when he is committed to one who really believes she is wronged. And that is what all women believe.

What shall I say of their ways? If I should attempt to show how often and to what extent they are inimical to the peace and repose of men, I should prolong my essay too much. So it must suffice to mention one trait common to almost all. They think that good conduct on the part of the lowest servant gives sufficient reason to retain him in a house, and the opposite conduct sufficient reason to dismiss him. Therefore they think that, if they themselves do well, their lot is no different from that of a servant, and they believe that they are ladies only when, notwithstanding bad conduct, they are not dismissed as servants are. Why should I state in detail that which most of us know? I judge that it is better to keep silent than to displease charming women by speaking. Who does not know that everything which is bought is tried by the purchaser before he buys it, except a wife? He may not see if she pleases him before he takes her home. Whoever takes a wife must have, not what he wants, but what Fortune grants him. And if what has been said above is true (and he who has experienced it knows), we can imagine what sorrow is concealed in rooms which from the outside, by those whose eyes cannot penetrate the walls, are reputed places of joy. Of course I do not affirm that these things fell to Dante's lot, for I do not know. However, it is true that either things of this sort or others must have been the reason why, when he was once parted from her who was given to him for the consolation of his grief, he never would come where she was, or allow her to come where he was, although he had been by her the father of several children. Let no one believe from what has been said above that I conclude that men should not marry. On the contrary, I recommend marriage, but not for all. Let philosophers leave marriage to the rich and foolish, to nobles and peasants, and let them take their delight with philosophy, a much better bride than any.

CHAPTER FOUR

Dante's family cares, honours, and exile

It is in the nature of temporal matters that one thing often leads to another. His family cares drew Dante to cares of state, in which the vain honours which are joined to public office so entangled him that, without noticing where he had started from or knowing where he was going, he gave himself up almost entirely, with loosened rein, to the government of the state. Fortune was, in this, so favourable to him that no embassy was heard or answered, no law passed or repealed, no peace made, no war begun, and in short, no discussion of any weight undertaken, unless he first gave his opinion with regard to it. In him seemed to rest the public faith and every hope; in him, in short, all things, both divine and human.

But Fortune, who overrides our plans and is the enemy of all human certainty, though she had kept him for some years in power and glory at the top of her wheel, at last brought him, when he trusted her too much, to an end very different from his beginning. In his time, the citizens of Florence were perversely divided into two parties, each of which was powerful through the efforts of its acute and sagacious leaders. Sometimes one party and sometimes the other ruled the city, and always for longer than pleased the defeated party. In the hope of uniting the divided body of his republic, Dante brought to bear all his genius, art, and learning, showing to the clearest-headed citizens how, by discord, great things in a short time come to nothing, and how by concord small things increase infinitely.

But when he saw his trouble was to no avail, and recognised that the minds of his hearers were obstinate, believing it all to be the will of God, he at first resolved to renounce all public offices and to live privately. Then, attracted by the sweetness of glory, the empty favour of the people, and the persuasions of his elders, he came to believe that, if the opportunity came to him, he could effect much more good for his city if he were deeply involved in public affairs than if he lived privately and took no share in them. O foolish desire for worldly splendour, how much greater is your strength than anyone can believe who has not experienced it! This mature man, brought up in the sacred bosom of philosophy, and nourished and taught there, who had in front of his eyes the fall of ancient and modern kings, the desolation of kingdoms, provinces, and cities, and the furious blows of Fortune, who sought nothing but the highest good, had not the knowledge or the power to protect himself from your charm!

So Dante decided to pursue the fleeting honours and vain pomp of public office. Seeing that by himself he could not form a third party, which by its very justice might defeat the injustice of the other two and restore them to unity, he attached himself to the party which in his judgement had most reason and justice on its side, and worked continually for that which he knew to be wholesome for his city and its citizens. But the plans of man are most often defeated by the powers of heaven. Hatred and animosity were engendered, although without just cause, and grew greater from day to day, so that, to the great confusion of the citizens, men often came to arms with the intention of putting an end to their quarrel by fire and sword. They were so blinded by their anger that they failed to see that they themselves must thus miserably perish. But after each of the parties had many times proved its strength with mutual loss, the time came when the secret designs of menacing Fortune would be disclosed. Rumour, who reports equally things false and true, announced that the adversaries of the party espoused by Dante were strong in marvellous and subtle plans and in a great multitude of armed men. Rumour thus so terrified the leaders among Dante's colleagues that she deprived them of all sense and all forethought, and every motive except that of seeking safety in flight. With them Dante, thrust down in an instant from the highest place in the city's government, saw himself not only fallen to earth, but thrust out from the city. Not many days after this, the mob having already rushed to the houses of the exiles and furiously gutted and ransacked them, the victors reorganised the city according to their will. All the leaders of the opposite party, and with them Dante (who was regarded not as one of the less important members, but as the chief almost) were, as principal enemies of the republic, condemned to perpetual exile, and their estates either confiscated for the public benefit, or appropriated by the victors.

This reward Dante received for the tender love he had for his country! This reward Dante received for his toil in trying to do away with public discord! This reward Dante received for having by all means possible sought the good, the peace, and the tranquillity of his fellow-citizens! It must thus be plainly manifest how deceptive are the favours of the people and what little trust can be put in them. He in whom, but a little while before, the city had placed all its faith and affection, and who was the people's refuge, was now suddenly, without just cause, without crime or fault, but by that Rumour who had many times before been heard bearing his praises to the stars, madly sent into irrevocable exile. This was the marble statue erected to the eternal memory of his virtue! With these letters was his name inscribed on tablets of gold among those of the fathers of the country! By such a favourable opinion were thanks returned him for his kindnesses! Who, considering these things, will say that our republic is not lame in this foot?

O vain confidence of mortal men, by what great examples are you continually reproved, admonished, and chastened! Ah, if Camillus, Rutilius, Coriolanus, both Scipios, and other ancient men of worth have escaped your memory because of the length of time that has intervened, this recent fall from favour should make you run after your pleasures in a more temperate way. Nothing has less stability than the favour of the people. No hope is more mad, no advice more insane than that which encourages people to put their trust in it. Let then our hearts be raised to heaven, in whose perpetual law, in whose eternal splendours, in whose true beauty can be clearly perceived the stability of Him who rules heaven and all heavenly things by His own purposes. Neglecting transitory things, may all our hope be directed to Him as to a fixed goal, and may we be not deceived.

CHAPTER FIVE

Dante's flight from Florence and his travels

That was how Dante departed from the city of which not only was he a citizen but his ancestors had been the rebuilders, leaving there his wife, together with the rest of his family, whose youth made them unable to flee. At ease about his wife, because of her relationship to one of the chiefs of the other party, but uncertain with regard to himself, he wandered here and there through Tuscany. His wife had, with difficulty, defended from the infuriated people a small portion of his property under the title of her dowry, and on the proceeds of this she managed to provide very simply for herself and her children. He, therefore, was forced in poverty to win his sustenance by himself by unaccustomed labour. Oh, what honest indignation he had to repress, more bitter to him than death, while hope promised him that his exile would be brief and his return speedy!

Against his expectation, however, he remained for many years (after leaving Verona, where in the first years of his flight he had gone to Alberto della Scala, by whom he had been kindly received) now with Count Salvatico in the Casentino, now with the Marchese Moruello Malaspina in Lunigiana, now with the della Faggiuola family in the mountains near Urbino, and always suitably honoured, as far as the times and as far as the means of his hosts permitted. Then he went to Bologna, where he stayed a little while, and then to Padua, from where he returned to Verona. But after he had seen the way closed on all sides against his return, and his hopes grew more vain from day to day, he left not only Tuscany but all Italy, crossed as best he could the mountains which separate it from the province of

Gaul, and went to Paris.

Here he gave himself up entirely to the study of philosophy and theology, revising also whatever of the other branches of knowledge his difficulties had made him forget. And while he thus spent his time in study, it happened, contrary to his expectation, that Henry, Count of Luxembourg, was, at the command and with the goodwill of Clement V, who was then Pope, elected King of the Romans, and then crowned Emperor. Dante, hearing that he had left Germany to subjugate Italy, which was in places rebellious against his majesty, and that he had already laid strong siege to Brescia, and expecting for many reasons that the Emperor would be victorious, conceived the hope that through the Emperor's power and justice he could return again to Florence, though he knew that Florence was against the Emperor.

Therefore, crossing the Alps again, Dante joined the enemies of the Florentines and their party, and by embassies and letters tried to draw the Emperor from the siege of Brescia, so that he might lay siege to Florence, as the chief of his enemies. Dante suggested that, if she were conquered, the Emperor would have little or no difficulty in attaining free and rapid possession and power over all Italy. But although he and others with the same purpose succeeded in drawing the Emperor there, his coming did not have the result they expected. The resistance was vigorous and much greater than they had anticipated. Therefore, without having accomplished anything in particular, the Emperor departed almost in despair, and turned towards Rome. And although in one way and another he accomplished much, brought order, and planned to do more, his too sudden death put an end to everything. At this, those who had expectations of him became generally discouraged, and especially Dante, who, without making further efforts to return to Florence, passed over the Appennines and went into Romagna, where his last day, which was to put an end to all his troubles, awaited him.

In those days the Lord of Ravenna, a famous and ancient city of Romagna, was a noble knight, whose name was Guido Novel da Polenta. Trained in liberal studies, he paid high honours to men of worth, and especially to those who surpassed others in knowledge. When he heard that Dante, beyond all expectation, was in Romagna in great despair, he decided (since he had long before known Dante's worth by repute) to receive and honour him. And he did not wait to be asked. With a generous mind, reflecting how men of worth must feel shame in asking favours, he approached Dante with offers, asking of Dante as a special favour that which he knew Dante must ask of him – that he would be pleased if he would reside with him. The two desires, that of the asker and of him who was asked, reached the same end, and Dante, being extremely pleased at the liberality of the noble knight, and also being constrained by necessity, went to Ravenna without waiting to be asked twice. There he was honourably received by the knight, who revived with kindly encouragement his failing hopes, gave him in abundance all that he needed, and kept him there for many years, indeed to the end of his life.

No loving desires, nor tears of grief, nor household cares, nor the tempting glory of public office, nor miserable exile, nor intolerable poverty had the power to divert Dante ever from his principal intent – his sacred studies. For, as will later be seen when his works are treated separately, in the midst of the fiercest passions mentioned above he exercised himself in poetry and philosophical studies. And if, in spite of all those obstacles which have been mentioned, he by dint of intellect and perseverance became as illustrious as we see him to be, what might he have become if he had had as much to help him, or nothing working against him, or very few hindrances, as many have? Surely, I do not know, but if it were proper to say so, I should say that he would have become a god on earth.

CHAPTER SIX

His death and funeral honours

With all hope of ever returning to Florence lost, although the desire itself was not lost, Dante then lived for many years in Ravenna under the protection of this gracious lord. Here by his teaching he trained many scholars in poetry, and especially in the vulgar tongue, which, according to my judgement, he was the first to exalt and make esteemed among us Italians, precisely as Homer made his tongue esteemed among the Greeks, and Virgil his among the Latins. Before him, although we must admit that it had been invented only recently, there was no one who had the sensitivity and the boldness to make the language the medium of any serious matter by numbering the syllables and by ensuring the consonance of the line endings. Rather they only exercised themselves in it on love trifles. He showed by his results that any lofty matter could be treated in it, and made our vulgar tongue glorious above all others.

But the allotted hour comes to all. Dante, having about the middle of his fifty-sixth year fallen sick, received all the sacraments of the Church, according to the Christian religion, humbly and with devotion, and reconciled himself to God in contrition for all that he had committed against His will as a mortal. In the month of September in the year of our Lord 1321, on the day that the exaltation of the holy cross is celebrated by the Church, to the great sorrow of Guido da Polenta and of all the other citizens of Ravenna, he rendered up to his creator his wearied spirit. I have no doubt he was received into the arms of his noble Beatrice, with whom, in the sight of Him who is the highest good, with all the miseries of the present life left behind, he now lives most joyfully in that life whose happiness shall never end.

The generous knight had the dead body of Dante placed upon a funeral bier adorned with poetic tributes, and he had this borne upon the shoulders of the most illustrious citizens to the place of the Friars Minor in Ravenna, with the honour that he thought due to such a body. When it had been followed there by public lamentation, he had it placed in the stone sarcophagus in which it still lies. And returning to the house in which Dante had lived, he himself, according to the custom in Ravenna, made a long and eloquent address, to commend the high learning and virtue of the deceased and to console the friends whom he had left behind in this sorrowful life. He also intended, if his life and power had lasted, to honour him with such a distinguished tomb that, if no other merit had rendered him memorable to posterity, this would have done so.

This praiseworthy proposal was quickly made known to many who at that time were distinguished poets in Romagna. All of them, both to show their own skill and to bear witness to the goodwill borne by them to the dead poet, and to win the favour and love of their lord, who they knew desired it, wrote laudatory verses which, placed as an epitaph on the proposed tomb, would indicate to posterity who lay in it. These poems they sent to the noble lord, who, by great misfortune, lost his power, and not long after died at Bologna, for which reason both the making of the tomb and the inscribing on it of the verses sent him were left undone. These verses were shown to me long afterwards, and since they were not used because of the accident already mentioned, and believing that what I am now writing, although not a material tomb, still may serve, as that would have served, to preserve his memory forever, I judge it not inappropriate to add them here. But since only one of those which were written (and they were many) would have been inscribed on the marble, so I think only one of them is needed here. Having examined them all, I find the most worthy in form and sense to be the fourteen lines by Master Giovanni del Virgilio of Bologna, then a great and famous poet and an intimate friend of Dante. These are the lines:

Dante, well versed in all theology,
All wisdom fostered by philosophy,
The Muses' joy, yet pleasing to the crowd,
Lies here: his high repute spreads far and wide.
He placed the dead precisely with twin swords:
Our common tongue and high-resounding words.
The pastures echoed to his rustic oat,
Until black Atropos cut his thread short.
Ungrateful Florence, harsh to her own son,
Sent him to exile, never to return:
Kind Ravenna is happy that he stayed
Under the aegis of her honoured lord.
In the year thirteen twenty-one he was
Borne back in glory to his native stars.

CHAPTER SEVEN

The Florentines reproached

Oh, ungrateful country, what madness, what negligence possessed you, when with unaccustomed cruelty you put to flight your dearest citizen, your eminent benefactor, your only poet? What possessed you subsequently? If you perhaps excuse yourself by the general madness of the moment, induced by evil counsel, why, when anger had passed away, and tranquillity of mind was restored, did you not repent of the deed and recall him? Ah, do not be unwilling to be judged by me, your son, but take what just indignation makes me say as from a man who desires you should amend, and not that you should be punished. Do you think that you had such titles to glory that you should deliberately exile one the like of whom no neighbour city can boast? Ah, tell me, what victories, what triumphs, what excellencies, what worthy citizens can you boast? Your riches, which are unstable and uncertain, your beauties, which are fragile and failing, your high standard of living, which is blameworthy and effeminate, have made you famous in the false judgement of the crowd, which always looks more to appearance than to reality. Will you glory in your merchants and in the artists in whom you abound? You will be foolish to do so. The former, in their constant avarice, ply a servile trade. Artistry, which was once ennobled by geniuses, in that they made it a second Nature, is now itself corrupted by avarice, and is worthless. Will you glory in the cowardice and sloth of those who, because they can bring to mind their many ancestors, wish to gain the headship of your nobility, and always by robbery and treachery and deceit? Your glory will be in vain, and you will be scorned by those whose judgements have a proper basis and real stability.

Ah, wretched mother, open your eyes and see with some remorse what you did. At least be ashamed that, although you are reputed to be wise, you made a bad choice! If you did not in yourself have such good judgement, why did you not imitate those cities which are still famous for their praiseworthy works? There was Athens, which was one of the jewels of Greece, at that time monarch of the world, splendid in knowledge, eloquence, and warfare; Argos still glorious for her kings; Smyrna, always revered by us for Nicholas her bishop; Pylos, renowned for the aged Nestor; and Chyme, Chios, and Colophon, splendid cities of the past. None of them, while they were most glorious, was ashamed of the divine poet Homer. They did not hesitate to dispute sharply over his origin, each affirming that he came from her; and each made her claim so strong by argument that the dispute still lasts. It is still uncertain where he came from, because they all still glory in this citizen. And Mantua, our neighbour, gains all her fame from the fact that Virgil was a Mantuan. They still revere his name, and he is so acceptable to everyone that his image is not only in many public but also in many private places, showing that, although his father was a potter, he has ennobled them all. Sulmona glories in Ovid, Venosa in Horace, Aquino in Juvenal, and many others glory in their sons, and argue over their greatness. It would have been no shame for you to follow the example of these cities, since it is improbable that without reason they would have been so fondly tender of such citizens. They knew what you yourself could have known and still may. I mean that the unceasing influence of such sons would, even after their cities' ruin, still keep their cities' names eternal, just as at present, spread through all the world, it makes them known to men who have never seen them.

Only you, overshadowed by some blindness, have wished to follow another course, and, as if you were illustrious in yourself, have had no care for this splendour. Only you, as if the Camilli, the Publicoli, the Torquati, the Fabricii, the Fabii, the Catos, and the Scipios had been your citizens and by their magnificent deeds had made you famous, have not only let your ancient citizen and poet Claudian fall from your hands, but have not taken care of the present poet. Indeed, you have chased him away, banished him, and would have deprived him, if possible, of your name. I cannot escape being ashamed on your behalf. But look! Not Fortune, but the natural course of things has so far favoured unworthy desire, that what you in your brutal eagerness would have done yourself if he had fallen into your hands – that is, killed him – it has accomplished by its eternal law. Your Dante Alighieri lies dead in that exile to which, envious of his worth, you unjustly condemned him. Oh, it is a crime best forgotten that a mother should be envious of the virtues of her son. Now you are free from worry, now through his death you live secure in your faults, and can put an end to your long and unjust persecution. He cannot do against you, now that he is dead, that which living he never would have done. He sleeps under another sky than yours, and you may never think to see him again, except on that day when you will see all your citizens, and see their sins weighed and punished by a just judge.

If, then, hatred, anger, and ill feeling cease, as may well be thought, at the death of anyone, come back to yourself and to your right mind. Start to be ashamed of having acted contrary to your ancient humanity. Start to look like a mother and no longer a foe. Pay your son his debt of tears. Give him your motherly pity. At least recover him dead whom you refused, indeed expelled as a suspect, when alive. Restore to his memory your citizenship, your welcome, your grace. In truth, however ungrateful and insolent you were towards him, he always as a son held you in reverence, and never would deprive you of the honour that should come to you through his works, as you deprived him of your citizenship. Although his exile was long, he always called himself a Florentine, and desired to be so called. He always preferred you to every other city. He always loved you.

What, then, will you do? Will you always persist in your iniquity? Shall there be less humanity in you than in the barbarians whom we find not only demanding back the bodies of their dead, but ready to die like men for the sake of possessing them? You wish the world to believe you the granddaughter of Troy the famous, and daughter of Rome. Surely children should resemble their fathers and grandfathers? Priam, in his grief, not only demanded back the body of the dead Hector, but bought it back with much gold. The Romans, as some believe, brought back from Miturnum the bones of the first Scipio, which he had at his death with good reason forbidden them. And, although Hector was for a long time by his prowess the defence of the Trojans, and Scipio the liberator not only of Rome but of all Italy (neither of which services could properly be credited to Dante) Dante is not therefore to be neglected, for never yet have arms failed to give place to learning. If you did not at first, and when it would have been most fitting, imitate the example and the deeds of the wise cities, mend your ways now and follow them. None of the seven Greek cities I have mentioned failed to erect for Homer a real or supposed tomb. And who doubts that the Mantuans, who still honour the fields and the poor cottage in Pietola that were Virgil's, would not have erected him an honourable tomb if Octavian Augustus, who had transported

37

his bones from Brindisi to Naples, had not ordered that they should forever remain in peace where he had placed them? Sulmona long grieved for nothing other than that her Ovid lay in an unknown grave in the land of Pontus. Similarly, Parma rejoices in her possession of Cassius. You too should seek to be the guardian of your Dante. Beg him back. Show your humanity, even if you do not have any desire to regain him. By this fiction rid yourself of some of the blame that you have had so long. Beg him back. I am sure that he will not be restored to you, and you can show yourself to be kind, and at the same time delight, when you do not recover him, in your innate cruelty. But why do I go on urging you? I find it hard to believe that, if dead bodies had feeling, Dante's would depart from where it is, to return to you. He lies with company far more honourable than that which you could give him. He lies in Ravenna, in age far more venerable than you. And although in old age she is rather ugly, she was in her youth far more flourishing than you. She is almost one general tomb of sacred bodies, and one cannot take a step there without treading on venerable ashes. Who, then, would desire to return to you, to lie among your ashes, which may be thought to preserve still the rage and iniquity that were theirs in life, and which, on bad terms with each other, flee from one another, as did the flames of the two Thebans? And, although Ravenna was once bathed in the precious blood of many martyrs, and today with reverence preserves their relics, and similarly the bodies of many magnificent emperors and others illustrious for their ancestors and their virtuous deeds, she rejoices not a little in having been granted by God, besides her other gifts, the privilege of being the perpetual guardian of such a treasure as is the body of him whose works hold the whole world in admiration, and of whom you have not been worthy. But surely the joy of having him is not so great as the envy that she bears you for having the right to his birth, almost disdaining the fact that she will be remembered for his last days, while beside her you will be named for his first. Remain therefore in your ingratitude, and allow happy Ravenna to glory forever in your honours!

CHAPTER EIGHT

Dante's appearance, way of life, and habits

The end of Dante's life, such as I have described, was worn out by various studies. Since I feel I have sufficiently described his love, his domestic and public cares, his miserable exile, and his end, in accordance with my promise, I now consider it proper to go on to speak of his bodily stature, of his clothes, and in general of his more notable habits. Then I shall pass straightaway from these to those works worthy of note which he composed in his day, a day troubled by such a storm as has been briefly shown above.

Our poet then was of medium height, and after he came to maturity he bent somewhat as he walked, and his gait was grave and gentle. He was always dressed in good clothes of a fashion appropriate to his years. His face was long, his nose aquiline, his eyes rather big, his jaw large, and his lower lip protruded beyond the upper. His complexion was dark, his hair and beard thick, black, and curly, and his expression was melancholy and thoughtful.

It happened one day at Verona – when the fame of his works was already widely spread, and especially of that part of his *Comedy* which he calls the *Inferno*, and when he was known by many, both men and women – that, passing before a door where many women were sitting, one of them said softly to the others (but not so softly that she was not clearly heard by him and by his companion), 'Do you see the man who goes to hell, and returns when he pleases, and brings back news of those who are below?' To this one of the others responded naively, 'Indeed, you must be speaking the truth. Don't you see how his beard is crisped and his complexion browned by the heat and smoke that is below?' Hearing these words said behind him, and knowing that they came from the women's simple belief, he was pleased, and passed on, smiling a little, as if content that they thought this.

In his domestic and public habits he was admirably orderly and self-contained, and in all things he was more courteous and civil than others.

In food and drink he was temperate, both in taking them at regular hours, and in not taking more than necessary. He did not have any special taste for one thing more than for another. He praised delicate viands, but for the most part ate plain food, condemning strongly those who made great efforts to get choice things and have them prepared with great care, declaring that such eat not to live, but rather live to eat.

No one was more scrupulous than he, whether wrestling with his studies or with other problems, so that his family and his wife were often disturbed by it, until they grew used to his ways and paid no attention to it.

He rarely spoke when not questioned, and then thought-fully and in a tone appropriate to the matter of which he spoke. When it was necessary, however, he was eloquent and fluent, with an excellent and ready delivery.

In his youth he was extremely fond of music and singing, and he was friend and companion of every one of the best singers and players of those times. Often his love for music incited him to compose poems, which he had his friends clothe in pleasing and masterly melody.

How fervently he was subject to love has already been clearly shown. It is everyone's firm belief that this love moved his genius to become a poet in the vulgar tongue, at first through imitation, and afterwards through a desire for glory and to set forth his emotions more impressively. He took great

pains in composition, and not only surpassed all his contemporaries, but so clarified and beautified the Italian tongue
that he made many then and after him (as he will in future)
desirous of becoming expert in verse.

He was especially fond of being alone, and at a distance
from people, in order that his contemplations might not be
interrupted. If any thought that greatly pleased him came to
him while he was in company, no matter what was asked him,
he would never respond to the questioner until he had either
accepted or rejected this thought. This happened many times,
when he was questioned while at table or journeying in
company, or elsewhere.

In his studies he was most assiduous, both in regard to the
time which he gave up to them, and in the fact that no news
that he heard could withdraw his attention from them. It is
credibly reported of this habit of his of giving himself up
entirely to whatever pleased him, that once he was in Siena,
and happened by chance to be in an apothecary's shop, and
a book which had been promised him and which was very
famous among experts, but which he had never seen, was
brought to him. Not having the opportunity to take it away, he
leaned his breast against a bench in front of the apothecary's,
and put the book there, and began to examine it eagerly. And
although a little later there was a grand tournament of young
gentlemen in that district for some great celebration of the
Sienese, and the bystanders made a great deal of noise (as they
are accustomed in such cases to do, with applauding cries
and various instruments), and although enough other things
happened to attract the attention of anyone else (dancing,
for instance, by beautiful women, and many youthful sports)
there was no one who saw him stir or once lift his eyes from
the book. Indeed, it was about midday when he took up his

position there, and it was in the evening, by which time he had read the whole book and understood the gist of it, when he arose from it. Afterwards, he affirmed, to some who asked him how he could keep from looking at such a fine celebration as was carried on in front of him, that he had heard nothing of it. Thus, to the questioners, a second cause for wonder was, with good reason, added to the first.

This poet had also wonderful ability, a retentive memory, and a penetrating intellect – so much so that, being in Paris, and there playing the part of a proposer, in a disputation *de quolibet* which was held in the schools of theology, of fourteen theses of various kinds, brought forward by various worthy men, he without a break gathered in the arguments for and against, and recited them in the same order in which they had been given, acutely analysing and replying to the contrary arguments. This was a feat which was thought almost a miracle by the bystanders.

He also had a lofty genius and acute powers of literary invention, as his works make more clear to his readers than my words ever could. He was eager for honour and glory, perhaps more eager than befitted his illustrious virtue. But what then? What life is so humble that it is not touched by the sweetness of glory? It was because of this desire, I believe, that he loved poetry more than any other study, seeing that, although philosophy surpasses all the others in nobility, its excellence can be communicated only to a few, and many are famous throughout the world for distinction in it, whereas poetry is more comprehensible and delightful to everyone, and poets are rare. He hoped, moreover, through poetry to attain to the rare and distinguished honour of being crowned with the laurel, and so gave himself up to study and composition. His desire would certainly have been fulfilled if Fortune had been so gracious to him as to allow him ever to return to Florence, where he wished to be crowned at the font of St John, in order that here, where he had received his first name in baptism, he should by that coronation receive his second name of poet. But, as it turned out, although his title was clear, and he could have had, anywhere else he pleased, the honour of receiving the laurel (which, though it does not increase knowledge, is its ornament and a sure token of its acquisition), in his desire to return where he could never be, he was unwilling to receive it elsewhere. So he died without the much coveted honour.

Now, since people often ask what poetry is and what poets are, and where the words come from, and why poets are crowned with laurel, and these matters seem to have been explained by few, I wish to make a digression here, in which I shall to some extent clarify this matter, returning to my main theme as soon as possible.

CHAPTER NINE

Digression with regard to poetry

The first peoples in the first centuries, although they were very rough and uncivilised, were exceedingly eager to find out the truth by study, just as we now see everyone naturally desires this. Seeing the heavens moving continually in accordance with fixed laws, and earthly things with their fixed order and various functions at various times, they thought there must be something from which these things proceeded, and which, as a superior power, governed all the other things and was not governed itself. And after diligent thought they imagined that this thing, which they called divinity or deity, was to be cultivated, venerated, and honoured with more than human service. Therefore they built, in reverence to the name of this great power, large and distinguished edifices. They thought that these should be separated by name as they were in form from those in which people generally lived, and they called them temples.

Similarly they appointed various ministers, who were sacred and relieved from worldly care, and could devote themselves entirely to divine service, and were in maturity and age and habits more respected than other men, and these they called priests. Furthermore, they made, in representation of the imagined divine essence, magnificent statues of various forms, and for their service, vessels of gold and marble tables and purple vestments and all the other apparatus necessary for the sacrifices established for them. And in order that to so great a power a silent and a mute honour might not be paid, it seemed to them that they should humble themselves before it with words of lofty sound, and render it propitious to their needs. And as they thought that this power exceeded everything else in nobility, they wished to find words far from the ordinary plebeian or public style of speaking, and worthy of the divinity, in which they could offer their sacred praise. Moreover, in order that these words might seem to have more efficacy, they wanted them composed according to laws of rhythm, by which pleasure might be felt and resentment and annoyance removed. And it was clearly appropriate that this should be done, not in a vulgar or accustomed form of speech, but in one that was artistic, exquisite, and unusual. This form the Greeks called *poetes*. So it arose that what was made in this form was called *poesis*, and those who made or used such a manner of speaking were called *poets*. This, then, was the origin of the name of poetry, and consequently of poets. Others argue differently, and perhaps rightly, but this notion pleases me most.

This good and praiseworthy intention of that uncivilised age moved many people to invent new gods, as the world's knowledge grew. While the early people honoured one deity alone, their successors believed there were many, although they said that one held primacy over the others. These many deities they thought were the Sun, the Moon, Saturn, Jove, and each of the other seven planets, and they proved the deity of these by their influence. Hence they came to show that everything that was useful to men was a deity, even if it were an earthly thing, like fire, water, earth and the like. To all these they paid honour and made verses and established sacrifices. Then various men in various places, one by one talent and one by another, began successively to rise above the unlearned multitude of their districts, deciding rough disputes not according to written law, for they had none yet, but according to a natural sense of justice, with which one was more endowed than another. Being more enlightened by nature itself, they imposed order on their lives and customs, resisting by physical force any opposition that might arise. They began also to call themselves kings, and to show themselves to the people with slaves and ornaments not previously used by men, and to make themselves obeyed, and lastly to make themselves worshipped.

Once there was someone who had conceived the idea, this came about without much difficulty, because to such primitive peoples they seemed not men but gods. These men, not trusting too much in their strength, began to reinforce the feeling for religion, and by faith in it to frighten their subjects and to bind to obedience with sacraments those whom they could not have bound by force. And furthermore they took care to deify their fathers, their grandfathers, and their ancestors, in order to be more feared and held in reverence by the people. These things could not easily be done without the work of poets, who helped them by spreading their fame, by pleasing the princes, by delighting their subjects, and by persuading all to act virtuously. That which if spoken openly would have defeated their ends, but which the princes wished to have believed, they made the people believe by masterly fictions, such as are hardly understood by the uneducated now, not to mention then. For the new gods and for the men who pretended to be the descendants of gods, they used the same style that the early peoples had used only for the worship of the true God and for venerating Him. Then they came to equate the deeds of strong men with those of gods, and so arose the practice of celebrating in exalted verse the battles and other notable deeds of men together with those of gods. This was, and is today, together with the other things mentioned previously, the office and practice of all poets. And since many of little understanding do not believe that poetry is anything more than the telling of fables, I wish to go beyond my plan and show here briefly that poetry is theology, before I come to tell why poets are crowned with laurel.

If we would put our minds to it, and look at it rationally, I believe that we could easily see that the ancient poets followed, as far as the human mind can, the steps of the Holy Spirit. As we see in the divine Scripture, the Holy Spirit revealed to future times its highest secrets by many different mouths, making them utter under a veil that which at the proper time it intended to show, by works, without a veil. If we look at their works carefully, the poets, in order that they might not seem different from Holy Scripture, which they were imitating, described under the cover of some fiction that which had been, or was at that time, or which they desired or which they supposed should happen in the future. Therefore, although the two forms of writing do not look to the same end, but only to a single method of treatment (which most occupies my mind at present), they may both be given the same praise, using the words of Pope Gregory the Great. He said of Holy Scripture what may still be said of poetry, that in the same narrative passage it reveals the text and a mystery beneath it. It then, at the same time, with the one exercises the minds of the wise, and with the other comforts the simple. On the surface it nourishes children, and secretly it serves this end: that it holds the minds of lofty thinkers rapt in admiration. It is therefore, if I may say so, a river, gentle and deep, in which the little lamb may wade and the great elephant may easily swim.

But we must now proceed to the verification of what I have proposed.

CHAPTER TEN

The difference that exists between poetry and theology

Divine Scripture, which we call theology, sometimes under the guise of history, sometimes as if by a vision, sometimes in the form of a lament, or in many other ways, endeavours to show us the high mystery of the incarnation of the Divine Word. It shows us His life, the events which occurred at His death, His victorious resurrection, and His wonderful ascension, and all His other acts, through which we, taught by Him, may attain to that glory which He by His death and resurrection opened for us, after it had long been closed to us by the sin of the first man. So poets in their works, which we call *poetry*, sometimes by fictions of various gods, sometimes by the transformation of men into various shapes, sometimes by gentle persuasion, show us the reason of things, the results of virtues and vices, and what we should flee and what we should follow, in order that we may come by virtuous action to that end which they, although they did not really know the true God, believed our highest good. The Holy Spirit wished to show, by means of the green bush in which Moses saw God like an ardent flame, the virginity of her who was purer than all other creatures, and who was destined to be the receptacle and habitation of the Lord of Nature, and who was not to be contaminated by her conception, or by giving birth to the Word of the Father. It wished to show, by the vision seen by Nebuchadnezzar of the statue of many metals, which was destroyed by a stone turned into a mountain, that all past ages should be overwhelmed by the teachings of Christ, who was and is the living rock, and that the Christian religion, born of this rock, should become a thing as immovable and perpetual as the mountains which we see. It wished in the 'Lamentations of Jeremiah' to foretell the future destruction of Jerusalem.

In the same way, our poets, feigning that Saturn had many children and devoured all but four, intended by this fiction to make us believe nothing other than that Saturn is time, in which everything is produced, and just as everything is produced in time, so time corrupts all things and reduces them to nothing. Of the four children not devoured by him, one is Jove, that is to say the element of fire. The second is Juno, wife and sister of Jove, that is the air, by means of which fire works its effects below. The third is Neptune, the god of the sea, that is the element of water. The fourth and last is Pluto, the god of hell, that is the earth, which is lower than any other element. In the same way, our poets feigned that Hercules was transformed from a man into a god, and Lycaon from a man into a wolf. They wished in that way to teach us the moral lesson that, by such virtuous deeds as Hercules performed, man becomes a god and lives in heaven, and by such vicious deeds as Lycaon did, although he seems to be a man, in truth he can be said to be that beast which is known by all as having the effect most similar to his defect, for Lycaon, by rapacity and avarice, which are very appropriate for a wolf, is represented as changing into a wolf. In the same way, our poets imagined the beauty of the Elysian Fields, which I take to mean the sweetness of paradise, and the darkness of Dis, by which I understand the bitterness of hell, in order that we, attracted by the pleasure of the one and terrified by the suffering of the other, may follow the virtues that will lead us to Elysium, and flee the vices which would cause us to fall into Dis. I shall not go into more detail on these matters, for, although I should like to make them as clear as possible, and although they would become more pleasing and would greatly aid my argument, I do not doubt that they would lead me further than my main subject requires, and further than I am willing to go.

Surely, if I should say no more than has been said, it could be easily understood that theology and poetry agree with regard to the way they work. However, I say also that with regard to their subjects they are not only very different, but, in certain respects, opposite. The subject of sacred theology is divine truth, while that of the ancient poets is men and the gods of the pagans. They are opposite in as far as theology presupposes nothing which is not true, while poetry presupposes some things as true which are most false and erroneous and contrary to the Christian religion. But since some fools have risen up against the poets, saying that they have composed indecent fables, not consonant with the truth, and that in other ways than by fables they ought to have shown their powers and given their teaching to ignorant men, I wish to proceed still further with the present explanation.

Let such people, then, look at the visions of Daniel, of Isaiah, of Ezekiel, and of others described in the Old Testament by the divine pen, and explained there by Him who has neither beginning nor end. Let them look also in the New Testament at the visions of St John the Evangelist, full of admirable truth to those who understand them. Even if no poetic fable is found so far from truth and verisimilitude as these appear in many places outwardly, it must at least be conceded that poets have told fables calculated to give neither pleasure nor profit. Without saying anything of the blame which is laid on the poets for showing their teaching in fables or by fables, I could pass on, knowing that when people madly blame the poets for this, they incautiously fall into blaming that Spirit which is nothing else than the way, the truth and the life. But I wish to make a satisfactory explanation of it all.

It is obvious that everything that is acquired with toil has more sweetness in it than that which comes without trouble. The plain truth, because it is so quickly understood with little effort, delights us, and is forgotten. So, in order that truth acquired by toil should be more pleasing and that it should be better preserved, the poets concealed it under matters that appeared to be wholly contrary to it. They chose fables, rather than any other form of concealment, because their beauty attracts those whom neither philosophic demonstrations nor persuasions could have touched. What then shall we say of poets? Shall we suppose that they are madmen, like those carping fools, speaking and not knowing what they say? On the contrary, they are profoundly intelligent in their methods, as regards the hidden fruit, and of an excellent and beautiful eloquence as regards the bark and visible leaves. But let us return to where we left off.

I say that theology and poetry may be said to be almost one thing when the subject is the same. I say further that theology is nothing else than a piece of God's poetry. What other thing is it than poetic fiction in Scripture when Christ says that He is now a lion, and now a lamb, and now a serpent, and then a dragon, and then a rock, and when He speaks in many other ways, to recount all of which would be tedious? What else do the words of the Saviour in the gospels contain if not a meaning different from the plain sense, a way of speaking which we call by the common term allegory? It then clearly appears not only that poetry is theology, but that theology is poetry. Even if my words deserve little faith in so great a matter I shall not be disturbed. Believe Aristotle rather, a most worthy authority for matters of weight, who affirms that he has found that poets are the first theologians. Let this be enough on this subject, and let us turn to showing why to poets alone, among all men of knowledge, the honour of the laurel crown has been granted.

CHAPTER ELEVEN

The laurel bestowed on poets

Among the many nations which are on the surface of the earth, it is believed that the Greeks are those to whom philosophy first revealed itself and its secrets. From its treasures they drew military knowledge, and their understanding of political life and of many other important matters, through which they became more famous and celebrated than any other nation. Among other things drawn by them from that treasure was the sacred opinion of Solon cited at the beginning of this little work, and in order that their republic, which was then more flourishing than any other, should walk straight and stand on its own two feet, they arranged and observed a magnificent system of punishments for the wicked and of rewards for the good. Among the rewards established by them for well-doing this was the chief – to crown with laurel leaves, in public, and with the public consent, poets after their victorious toil, and emperors who had victoriously increased the power of the state. They considered that equal glory belonged to him by whose virtue human things were preserved and increased, and to him by whom divine matters were treated. Although the Greeks were the inventors of this honour, it passed over to the Romans when glory and arms gave place throughout the world to the Roman name, and it still survives in the coronation of poets, although this rarely happens now. It will be interesting to see why for such a coronation the laurel rather than any other leaf should be chosen.

There are some who believe, because they know that Daphne was loved by Phoebus and turned into a laurel, and that Phoebus was the first author and the patron of poets, and also one who triumphed, that for love of these leaves he crowned his lyres and his triumphs with them. So men followed his example, and consequently that which was first done by Phoebus brought about the use of such coronations and the use of such leaves up to these days for poets and emperors. Certainly this opinion does not displease me, and I do not deny that it may have been so, but another reason especially intrigues me, which is this. Those who investigate the virtues of plants and their nature, hold that the laurel, among its other properties, has three which are especially notable and praiseworthy. The first is, as we know, that it never loses its greenness or its leaves. The second is that this tree has never been found struck by lightning, a phenomenon which we do not read of in the case of any other tree. The third is that it is very fragrant, as we are aware. The ancients, who were the inventors of this honour, believed these three properties were fitting for the virtuous deeds of poets and of victorious emperors. In the first place, the perpetual green-ness of these leaves shows, they say, the fame of their work – that is, that the works of these who are crowned with laurel, or shall be crowned in the future, shall exist forever. Then they think that their works are of such power that neither the fire of envy, nor the lightning of time, which consumes all else, shall ever be able to strike them, any more than the heavenly fire strikes that tree. They say further that their works will never by length of time become less graceful and pleasing to whoever hears them and reads them, but be always acceptable and fragrant. So it is appropriate for a crown of such leaves rather than of others to be made for such men, the effects of whose works, so far as we can see, suit it. Therefore, not without reason, our Dante fervently desired such an honour, or rather such a testimony of ability as that is to those who become worthy of having their brows thus adorned. But it is now time to return to the point from which we departed in this digression.

CHAPTER TWELVE

Qualities and defects of Dante

Our poet was, in addition to what has been said before, a man of lofty and very disdainful spirit. When one of his friends was trying to bring it about at the insistence of Dante's prayers that he could return to Florence, a thing which he desired above everything else, he found that he could not make any arrangement with those who had the government of the Republic in their hands, except on condition that Dante should remain in prison for a fixed period, and after that make an act of humiliation in our principal church at some public festival. Then he would become free and exempt from all the sentences previously passed upon him. This seemed to Dante to be a practice suitable only in the case of vile and infamous men, and not suitable for anyone else. So, in spite of his great desire, he chose to stay in exile rather than return home by such means. Oh, praiseworthy scorn of the magnanimous, how manfully you worked in repressing the ardent desire to return by a way unworthy of a man nourished in the bosom of philosophy!

He also set great store by himself and, as his contemporaries report, did not consider himself to be worth less than he was really worth. Among other occasions, this trait appeared once notably while he was with his faction at the head of the government of the Republic. The party that was out of power had, through Pope Boniface VIII, called a brother or rather relative of Philip, then King of France, whose name was Charles, to direct the affairs of our city. All the chiefs of Dante's party assembled in counsel to deal with this matter. Among other things, they decided that an embassy should be sent to the Pope, who was then in Rome, to induce him to prevent Charles' coming, or to make him come with the agreement of the party which was then ruling. When they had to decide who should be the chairman of this embassy, it was agreed by all that it should be Dante himself. To this appointment Dante, getting somewhat above himself, said, 'If I go, who stays? If I stay, who goes?' as if he were the only one of any worth among them all, and as if the others were of account through him alone. These words were heard and remembered, but that which followed from them has nothing to do with the present subject, and therefore I will leave it and pass on.

This able man was, moreover, strong through all his adversities. In one matter alone I am afraid I have to say that he was impatient, even passionate. After he went into exile, he had more to do with matters concerning political parties than was appropriate, and more than he was willing to have others know about. To show what party it was that he was so passionately and pertinaciously attached to, it seems to me that I should pursue this matter somewhat further. I believe that the just anger of God permitted, a long time ago, almost all Tuscany and Lombardy to be divided between two parties. How they got such names I do not know; but one was called the Guelph party, and the other the Ghibelline. And these two names were of such power and reverence in the foolish hearts of many that to defend the chosen one against the other it was not thought a hardship to lose one's goods and ultimately one's life if that was necessary. And under these names the Italian cities often sustained grievous oppression and vicissitudes, including, among the others, our city, which was the head, as it were, now of one, now of the other party, according to the changing minds of its citizens. So the ancestors of Dante as Guelphs were twice exiled by the Ghibellines, and he likewise as a Guelph held the reins of the Republic of Florence. He himself was exiled, as I have shown, not by Ghibellines but by Guelphs, and seeing that he could not return, he so changed his sentiments that no one was a fiercer Ghibelline and opponent of the Guelphs than he. And what I most blush about for the sake of his memory is that it is a matter of public repute in Bologna that any woman or child speaking of politics to the disadvantage of the Ghibelline party could move him to such a pitch of madness that he would have thrown stones if the speaker had not fallen silent. And this animosity continued until his death. Of course I am ashamed to be obliged to blot the fame of such a man by any defect, but the plan on which I am working requires it to some degree, because if I am silent about anything that was not praiseworthy in him, I shall destroy the faith of the reader in the praiseworthy virtues which I have already pointed out. I excuse myself, therefore, to him who by chance looks down on me with a disdainful eye from high heaven as I write this.

In the midst of such virtue and learning as has been shown above to have been in this marvellous poet, lust found a large place, and not only in his youth but also in his mature years. This vice, although it be natural and common and, as it were, necessary, cannot in truth be commended or even excused. But who among mortal men shall be a judge so just as to condemn it? Not I. Oh, what lack of firmness in men, what bestial appetite! What influence over us can women not have, if they choose, seeing that, without their choice, they have so much? They have charm, beauty, natural appetite, and many other things continually working for them in the hearts of men. To show that this is true, let us not adduce what Jove did for the sake of Europa, Hercules for Iole, and Paris for Helen, since, because these are the subject matter of poetry, many of little judgement would call them fables. But let us take instances which no one can deny. Was there at that time more than one woman in the world, when our first father (breaking the commandment given him from the very mouth of God) yielded to her persuasions? Certainly not. And David, although he had many women, once he had seen Bathsheba, through her forgot God, his kingdom, himself, and his honour, and became first an adulterer and then a murderer. What can we think he would have done if she had given him any command? And did not Solomon, to whose wisdom no one except the Son of God ever attained, forsake Him who had made him wise, and to please a woman kneel and worship Baal? What did Herod do? What did many others do, led by nothing but their pleasure? Therefore among so many and so great instances our poet can be allowed to pass, not excused, but accused with much less severity than if he had been alone. And let this account of his more noteworthy habits suffice for the present.

CHAPTER THIRTEEN

The different works written by Dante

This glorious poet composed in his time many works, of
which I believe it suitable that there should be an orderly
memorandum, in order that none of his may be attributed to
anyone else, or another's by chance be attributed to him. He
first, while his lamentation for the death of his Beatrice lasted,
in his twenty-sixth year, brought together, in a little volume
which he called *New Life*, certain short pieces, sonnets and
odes, marvellously beautiful, which he had written in rhyme at
various times previously. Before each he wrote in detail and in
their right order the reasons which had induced him to
compose it, and after each he noted the divisions of the work
that preceded. And although in his more mature years he was
very ashamed of having written this little book, nevertheless,
considering his youth, it is very pleasing and beautiful, especially in the eyes of the common people.

Some years after this compilation, looking down from the
summit of the government of the republic over which he
stood, he saw on a great scale, as one can from such places,
what the life of men was like, what the errors of the common
people were, how few men kept themselves apart from the
common crowd, and of what honour they were worthy, and
what shame those deserved who went with the crowd, whose
ambition he condemned even more than his own. Then there
came into his mind a lofty thought, by which he proposed at
once, that is in the same work, to show his own ability, to
punish the vicious with grievous pains, to honour the worthy
with great rewards, and to prepare eternal glory for himself.
And, as I have already shown that he placed poetry before all

other studies, he saw fit to compose a poetic work. Having long considered what he should do, in his thirty-fifth year he began to accomplish what he had premeditated – that is to punish and reward the lives of men according to their merits and in all their diversity. And since he recognised that life was of three sorts – vicious, leaving vices and moving towards virtue, and virtuous – so he divided his work admirably into three books, beginning with punishing the vicious, and ending with rewarding the virtuous, in a volume which he entitled *Comedy*. These three books he divided each into cantos, and the cantos into stanzas, as can be plainly seen. He composed it all in verse, in the vernacular, with such great art and order and beauty that there has been no one yet who could justly fault it in any respect. How subtly he wrote it throughout can be seen by those who have the ability to understand. But just as we see that great things cannot be comprehended in a short time, we must also know that an undertaking so high, so great and so elaborate (for it was to include, in rhymed verse in the vernacular, the acts of men and their deserts, poetically treated) could not be accomplished in a short time, and especially by a man who was troubled by many and various accidents of Fortune, all full of anguish, and envenomed with bitterness, as I have shown that Dante was. So from the hour at which, as I said above, he first devoted himself to this high work, the labour continued up to the end of his life. Nevertheless, he composed other works in the meanwhile, as will appear.

It will be relevant now to mention briefly some accidents that happened with regard to the beginning and the end of his greatest work.

CHAPTER FOURTEEN

*Some accidents that occurred in the course of
writing the* Divine Comedy

While Dante was intent on his glorious poetical work, and had
already composed seven cantos of the first part of it, which
he called *Inferno* (a subject never previously treated by a
Christian, only by pagans), there occurred the grievous
incident of his exile, or flight, as it should be called. On
account of this, abandoning his poem and everything else, he
wandered for many years, uncertain as to his plans, with
different friends and lords. But we most certainly ought to
believe that against what God ordains Fortune can oppose no
obstacle by which she can prevent its accomplishment, though
she can perhaps delay it. So it happened that someone
(searching for a necessary document among other things of
Dante's in certain chests that had been hastily rescued and
deposited in sacred places, at that time when the ungrateful
and disorderly mob, more eager for booty than for just
revenge, rushed tumultuously to the house) found those seven
cantos that had been composed by Dante. He read them,
not knowing what they were, with admiration, and, being
delighted with them, cleverly took them from the place where
they were, and brought them to a fellow-citizen of ours, whose
name was Dino Frescobaldi, a famous poet in Florence in
those times, and showed them to him. At the sight of them
Dino, a man of high intelligence, marvelled, no less than he
who had brought them to him, at their beautiful, polished, and
ornate style and at the profundity of the sense which he
discovered hidden under the fair covering of words. On this
account and on account of the place from which they had been

taken, Dino, like the man who brought them, realised they were a work of Dante's. Anxious that the work should not remain imperfect, although they could not by themselves determine how it should end, they discussed with each other how to discover where Dante was, and how to send him what they had found, so that, if possible, he might give to this fine beginning the end he had planned for it. Hearing that he was with the Marchese Moruello, they wrote not to Dante but to the Marchese, outlining their hopes, and sending the seven cantos. When the Marchese, a man of great understanding, saw them, he thought highly of them, and he showed them to Dante, asking him if he knew whose work they were. Dante recognised them at once and replied that they were his. Then the Marchese begged him to have the kindness not to leave so sublime a beginning without a satisfactory end. 'Of course,' said Dante, 'I believed that in my ruin these and many of my other books were lost, and on account of this belief and the multitude of other troubles that came upon me with my exile, I had completely abandoned the great vision I had of this work. However, since Fortune has unexpectedly given it back to me, and since you admire it, I shall try to recall my first conception, and proceed as I am granted the grace to do so.' And taking up, not without trouble after such an interval, the abandoned idea, he continued it with the words: *I say, continuing, that long before...* [2] Anyone who looks closely can clearly see there the join in the interrupted work.

The magnificent work was, then, begun again by Dante, but he did not, as many might think, conclude it without several further interruptions. Indeed often, when the gravity of events required, he put it aside for months and years, without being able to accomplish anything on it. Nor could he make such haste that he was able to publish all of it before death overtook him. It was his custom, when he had finished six or seven cantos or so, before anyone else saw them, to send them from wherever he was to Messer Can Grande della Scala, whom he revered beyond any other man. After they had been seen by him, he made a copy for whoever wished one. In this manner, at the time of his death he had sent all except the last thirteen cantos. He had written them but not told anyone of their existence. The sons and disciples he left behind searched again and again for several months among all his manuscripts to see if he had written any conclusion to his work. Not managing to find the remaining cantos, all his friends were distressed that God had not at least lent him to the world long enough to complete what little remained to finish of his work. So they despaired of further searching and gave up.

Iacopo and Piero, sons of Dante, both of whom were poets, had resolved, on the persuasion of some of their friends, to finish their father's work, so far as they could, that it might not remain imperfect. Then to Iacopo, who was much more in earnest than the other, there appeared a marvellous vision, which not only destroyed his foolish presumption, but showed him where the thirteen cantos were which the *Divine Comedy* lacked and which they could not find. A worthy man of Ravenna, whose name was Piero Giardino, for a long time a disciple of Dante, has related that in the ninth month after the death of his master, Iacopo came to his house one night, near to the morning hour, and told him that that night, a short while previously, he had seen Dante, his father, come to him in his sleep, dressed in spotless clothes, and with an unusual light shining in his face. It seemed to him that he asked his father if he was alive and heard him reply that he was, but in the true life, not ours. It seemed to him also that he asked his father if he had completed his work before passing to the true life. If he had completed it, where was that which was lacking from it and which they had never been able to find? To this he seemed for a second time to hear a reply, 'Yes, I completed it.' And then it seemed that his father took him by the hand, and led him to the room where he was accustomed to sleep when he lived in this life, and touched a spot there, and said, 'That which you have so much sought after is here.' And once these words were said, it seemed to him that his sleep and Dante departed simultaneously. He said therefore that he had not been able to resist coming to bear witness to what he had seen, in order that together they might go to search in the place shown to him (which he had faithfully kept in mind), to see if a true spirit or a false delusion had pointed it out. So, with much of the night still remaining, they started together, went to the place mentioned, and there found a mat fixed to a wall. Gently lifting this, they saw a little opening, which neither of them had seen before or knew was there, and in it they found some writings, all mildewed by the dampness of the wall, and near to rotting had they stayed there only a little longer. Carefully cleaning the mildew from them, they read them, and saw they contained the thirteen cantos which they had so much sought. Therefore in great joy they copied them, and sent them first, according to the custom of the author, to Messer Can Grande, and then added them, as was only right, to the imperfect work. It was in this manner that the work, composed over many years, was completed.

CHAPTER FIFTEEN

Why the Comedy *is written in the vernacular*

Many people, with some wise men among them, tend to raise this point: since Dante was a distinguished man of learning, why did he decide to compose such a great and notable book, dealing with such high matters as his *Comedy*, in the Florentine idiom? Why not rather in Latin verse, as other poets had done before him? To this question I reply that there are many reasons, but two especially occur to me. Of these the first is that it was for the sake of being more useful to his fellow-citizens and other Italians. He knew that if he wrote Latin verse, as other poets had done previously, he would have been accessible only to the learned. If he wrote in the vulgar tongue he would accomplish something that had never been done before. This would not prevent its being understood by the learned, and would show the beauty of our language and his excellent skill in it, and give delight and understanding of himself to the unlearned who had, up to this point, been neglected by all. The second reason that led him to this conclusion was as follows. He saw that liberal studies had been neglected by all, and especially by princes and other great men to whom poetical works are customarily dedicated, and that therefore both the divine works of Virgil and those of other noted poets were not only held in slight esteem, but almost despised by the majority. He had begun, as his lofty subject demanded, in this fashion:

Ultima regna canam, fluvido contermina mundo,
spiritibus quae lata patent, quae premia solvunt
pro meritis cuicunque suis... [3]

There he stopped, for he thought it was useless to put crusts of bread into the mouths of those who were still sucking milk. So he began his work again in a style suited to modern taste, and continued it in the vernacular.

Some say he dedicated his *Comedy* to three illustrious Italians, to each one a part, in accordance with the book's division into three. The first part, *Hell*, he dedicated to Uguccione della Faggiuola, the then Lord of Pisa, who was famous in Tuscany. The second part, *Purgatory*, he dedicated to the Marchese Moruello Malaspina. The third part, *Paradise*, he dedicated to Frederick III, King of Sicily. Some say that he dedicated it all to Messer Can Grande della Scala. Which of these two suggestions is true we have no evidence of, except the gratuitous supposition of several people, and it is not a fact of such importance that it needs careful investigation.

CHAPTER SIXTEEN

The book of Monarchy *and other works*

This illustrious author also, at the coming of the Emperor Henry VII into Italy, wrote a book in Latin prose entitled *Monarchy*, which he divided into three parts in accordance with three points which he settled in it. In the first part, by logical arguments, he proves that the Empire is necessary to the well-being of the world, and this is the first point. In.the second, proceeding by historical arguments, he shows that Rome rightfully holds the title of the Empire, which is the second point. In the third, by theological arguments, he proves that the authority of the Empire proceeds directly from God, without the mediation of any vicar of His, as it seems that the clergy will have it, and this is the third point.

This book, some years after the death of its author, was condemned by Messer Beltrando, Cardinal of Poggetto and Legate of the Pope in Lombardy, while John XXII was Pope. The reason was that Ludwig, Duke of Bavaria, having been elected King of the Romans by the electors of Germany, came to Rome for his coronation against the wishes of Pope John. Then, being in Rome, against ecclesiastical ordinances he made a Friar Minor called Brother Piero della Corvara Pope, and appointed many cardinals and bishops, and had himself crowned there by this Pope. Then, when his authority began on many counts to be questioned, he and his followers, finding this book, began to use it to defend themselves and their authority with many of the arguments in it. Consequently the book, which up to this time was scarcely known, became very famous. Afterwards, when Ludwig had returned to Germany, and his followers, especially the clerics among them, were ruined and dispersed, Cardinal Beltrando, with no one to oppose him, seized the book and condemned it in public to the flames, as containing heretical matter. He tried also to burn the bones of the author, to the eternal infamy and shame of his own memory. He would have succeeded had he not been opposed by a noble and worthy Florentine knight, whose name was Pino della Tosa, who was then at Bologna where the discussion was carried on, and with him Messer Ostagio da Polenta, both of whom had influence over the Cardinal.

Besides his *Comedy* and *Monarchy*, Dante composed two beautiful eclogues, which were dedicated and sent by him, in response to certain verses, to Master Giovanni del Virgilio, whom I have mentioned above.

He also composed a commentary in prose, in the Florentine tongue, on three of his elaborate odes. He seems to have intended, when he began, to comment on them all, but afterwards, either through change of mind or for lack of time, he did not comment on more than these. This book he entitled *Banquet*. It is a very beautiful and praiseworthy little work.

Afterwards, when near to death, he composed a little book in Latin prose, which he entitled *On the Vulgar Tongue*, in which he intended to give instruction in the writing of vernacular verse to anyone who wanted it. Although he appears to have had in mind to compose four parts of this little book, either he did not do so before death overtook him, or the other parts were lost, for only two are extant.

This worthy poet also wrote many prose letters in Latin, of which some still survive. He composed many elaborate odes, sonnets, and other lyrics, both amorous and ethical, besides those which appear in his *New Life*, of none of which do I care to make special mention at present.

In such works as I have described above, this illustrious man consumed all the time which he could steal from his amorous sighs, his piteous tears, his private and public cares, and the various fluctuations of hostile fortune. These works are more acceptable to God and man than the deceit, fraud, lying, robbery, and treachery which the majority of men practise today, seeking by various ways the same goal, that of becoming rich, as if all success and honour and blessedness consisted in wealth. Oh, foolish minds! One brief fragment of an hour will separate the spirit from the failing body, and bring to nothing all these blameworthy toils, and time, which must consume all things, will either quickly destroy the memory of the wealthy man, or preserve it for a little while to his shame. This certainly will not happen to our poet. Rather, just as we see implements of war become more brilliant by usage, so will it be with his name, and the more it is rubbed by time, the more it will continue to shine. Therefore let him who wants to, toil on in his vain pursuits, and let it suffice him to be left alone to do so, without seeking to censure another's virtuous work, condemning things which he does not understand himself.

CHAPTER SEVENTEEN

Explanation of the dream of Dante's mother and conclusion

I have shown briefly the origin, studies, life, habits, and works of that great man and illustrious poet, Dante Alighieri, and made besides certain digressions, according as I have been permitted by Him who is the giver of every grace. I know that many others could have done it much better and with greater understanding, but no one is expected to do more than he is able. That I have written what I could will not serve as a bar to anyone else who believes that he can write better than I have done. Indeed, perhaps, if I have erred in any way, I shall, to tell the truth, give to another an occasion for writing about our Dante, which up to this time I find no one has done. But my task is not yet at an end. One part in the plan of the work which I promised remains for me to conclude. That is the dream of the mother of our poet, seen by her when she was pregnant with him. Of this I intend to deliver myself as briefly as I can, and bring my essay to an end.

The noble lady in her pregnancy saw herself at the foot of a lofty laurel, by a clear spring, give birth to a son, who, as I have said above, in a short time, feeding on the falling berries of that laurel and the water of the spring, became a great shepherd, and very hungry for the leaves of the laurel under which he was. When he tried to reach them, it seemed to her that he fell down, and suddenly she seemed to see, not him, but in his place a beautiful peacock. Disturbed by this marvel, the noble lady awoke from her sweet sleep without seeing more of him.

The divine goodness, which from all eternity, as well as now, foresees every future event, is of its own beneficence

72

accustomed, when nature, its general minister, is about to produce some unusual effect among mortals, to make us aware of it by some proof, either by signs or dreams, or in some other manner, in order that we may recognise by that forewarning that all knowledge of nature's products rests in the Lord. Such a sign, if we look clearly, was given in the coming into the world of the poet of whom so much has been said above. And to what person could this sign have been given who would have seen and observed it with so great affection as she who was to be the mother of the thing shown? Surely to no one other than to her. So God did show it to her, and what He showed her is already apparent to us from what I have said above. However, what God meant must be examined with a more careful eye. The lady, then, seemed to give birth to a son, which she did a short time after she saw the vision. But we still need to understand the significance of the lofty laurel under which she gave birth.

It is the opinion of astrologers and of many scientists that the influence of those higher bodies, the stars, produces, nourishes, and even, if the illuminating power of divine grace does not resist, guides inferior bodies. Therefore, since a superior body is most powerful in the degree to which it rises above the horizon in the hour when one is born, they say that the child is conditioned according to the qualities of that body. And so the laurel, under which the lady seemed to give our Dante to the world, means, I think, that the disposition of heaven at his nativity showed itself to be such that it foretold a great mind and poetic eloquence. These two things are signified by the laurel, the tree of Phoebus, with whose leaves poets are accustomed to be crowned, as has already been shown above. The berries from which the child took his nourishment I understand to be the effects which have already arisen from the disposition of heaven, which has been explained. These are poetical books and their teachings, by which works and teachings our Dante was most worthily nourished, that is to say, taught. The clear spring, of whose waters it seemed to her that he drank, means, I judge, nothing other than the richness of the teachings of moral and natural philosophy. Just as the spring proceeds from the hidden richness in the bowels of the earth, so these teachings have their essential nature and cause in copious demonstrative reasoning, which may be called the richness of the earth. And just as food cannot be well digested in the stomach of him who takes it, without drinking, so no knowledge can be well adapted to the intellect if it is not ordered and arranged by philosophic demonstrations. We may, therefore, well say that by the aid of the clear water (philosophy) he digested in his stomach (his intellect) the berries on which he fed (poetry) which, as I have mentioned, he studied with the greatest care.

His suddenly becoming a shepherd shows the excellence of his talent, because he suddenly became so great a man that in a short time he comprehended by study what was necessary for him in order to become a shepherd or pastor, a giver of food or pasture to other intellects that had need of it. As everyone may easily understand, there are two sorts of shepherds. There are the shepherds of the body and the shepherds of the soul. The shepherds of the body are of two sorts, of which the first are those who are commonly called shepherds, the guardians of the sheep and oxen and other animals. The second sort are the fathers of families, by whose care must be fed and guarded and ruled flocks of children and of servants and of others subject to them. The shepherds of the soul may also be said to be of two sorts. One consists of those who feed the souls of the living with the word of God. These are prelates, preachers, priests, to whose custody are committed the fragile souls of those who are assigned to them. The other sort is those who, by their great learning, either through interpreting what the ancients have written or writing in a fresh way what seems to them to have been omitted or not clearly explained, teach the souls and intellects of their hearers and readers. These are generally called doctors, whatever their branch of learning may be. Our poet quickly became a shepherd of this sort. If we ignore other works composed by him, the truth of this may be seen if we look at his *Comedy*. This, with the sweetness and beauty of its text, feeds not only men, but children and women, and, with the considerable charm of the profound meaning concealed in it, refreshes and feeds strong intellects, after holding them a while in suspense. His longing for the leaves of the tree whose fruit had nourished him, shows nothing else than his ardent desire, as has been said above, for the laurel crown, which is desired for no other reason than to bear witness to the fruit. She says that she saw him fall down while he was ardently desiring these leaves. This fall must be the fall which comes to everyone without their rising, that is death. And if we recall what has been said above, we know that death came upon him when he most desired his coronation.

She says next that she saw the shepherd suddenly become a peacock. By this change we may understand his posterity, which, although it consists also of his other works, lives especially in his *Comedy*, which, in my opinion, is very like the peacock, if we think of the characteristics of both. Among other characteristics the peacock apparently has four that are notable. The first is that he has angelic plumage, in which he has a hundred eyes. The second is that he has ugly feet and a noiseless tread. The third is that he has a very horrible voice. The fourth and last is that his flesh is fragrant and incorruptible. These four things our poet's *Comedy* clearly has in itself. However, since it is not convenient to follow the order in which they have been mentioned, I will take them in a different order, beginning with the last one.

I say that the meaning of our *Comedy* is like the flesh of the peacock, because, whether you call it moral or theological, it is, at whatever part of the work most pleases you, the simple and immutable truth, which not only cannot receive corruption, but, the more it is investigated, the greater the odour of incorruptible sweetness it gives off to its readers. Many examples could easily be given of this, if the present subject allowed. However, without mentioning any, I will leave the searching out of them to those who have understanding. Next, I say that angelic plumage covers this flesh. And I say angelic, not because I know that angels have any plumage of this sort or any other sort, but, conjecturing as mortals do, and hearing that they fly, I suppose that they must have feathers. Then, not knowing among our birds any with plumage more beautiful or exquisite, or so like the plumage of the peacock, I imagine the angels must have such plumage. Yet I do not name the plumage of the angels from that of the peacock, but the peacock's plumage from that of the angels, for the angel is a more noble bird than the peacock. By this plumage which covers the body, I understand the beauty of Dante's exquisite narrative, which is evident on the surface in the reading of the *Comedy*, as in his descending into hell and seeing the character of the place and the various conditions of the inhabitants, his ascending the mountain of purgatory and hearing the cries and laments of those who hope to be holy, and then his ascent into paradise and seeing the ineffable glory of the blessed. This is a narrative so beautiful and so exquisite that a more beautiful one was never conceived or heard of. The poem is divided into a hundred cantos, just as some hold that the peacock has in his tail a hundred eyes. These cantos distinguish the appropriate parts of the treatise as clearly as the eyes distinguish the colours and the diversity of objects. The flesh of our peacock is, therefore, clearly covered with angelic plumage.

In the same way the feet of this peacock are ugly and his tread soft, and these things correspond admirably with our author's *Comedy*. For just as it is evident that the whole body is supported by its feet, so it is immediately apparent that every work composed in writing is supported by its way of speaking, and the vernacular, in which and on which every joint of the *Comedy* is supported, is in comparison with that lofty and masterly literary style which every other poet uses, ugly, although it conforms more to the taste of today than those beautiful ones. His soft tread signifies the humility of the style, which is necessary in comedies, as those who understand what comedy means know.[4]

Finally, I say that the voice of the peacock is horrible, and this, although our poet's words are on the surface very pleasing, certainly corresponds very well with the *Comedy*, to one who considers the pith within. Who cries out more horribly than Dante, when with his bitter imagination he rebukes the faults of many living people, and chastises those of the dead? Whose voice is more horrible to him who is disposed to sin than the voice of him who chastens? No one's. With his images he at once terrifies the good and saddens the bad. Therefore, it appears, so far as this matter is concerned, that he can be said to have a voice that is truly horrible. For this reason and for the other reasons touched upon, it is apparent that he who when alive was a shepherd, after his death became a peacock, just as we may believe that it was, by divine inspiration, revealed in a dream to his dear mother.

I know that this is a very superficial exposition of the poet's mother's dream. There are several reasons for this. First, I had not perhaps the ability that is required for so great a task. Next, even granted that I had, my main theme would not permit it. Last, even if I had had the ability and the subject had permitted it, I should have done well not to say more than has been said, in order that something be left to be said by one with more ability than I and more desire. And so, now that I have said what seems to me to be enough, let whatever is lacking be left to the care of anyone who follows.

My little bark has now come to the port towards which it directed its prow when departing from the other shore. Although the voyage has been short, and the sea which it has furrowed shallow and calm, nevertheless, because it has arrived safely, I must render thanks to Him who has lent its sails a favourable breeze. To Him, with all the humility and devotion and affection that I possess, I render not such thanks as are deserved, but such as I can give, blessing forever His name and His worth.

NOTES

1. The name Dante is interpreted here as meaning 'he who gives', with particular reference to Dante's gift to us of the *Divine Comedy*.

2. This is the beginning of the eighth canto of the *Inferno*. With its reference to what has happened 'long before' the final incident of the previous canto, it uses a formula not found elsewhere in the *Divine Comedy*. This lends credence to Boccaccio's account.

3. I sing of those most distant realms which border on the world of the River of the Dead, spacious realms which lie open to souls and reward them all according to their merit…

4. For Boccaccio, and Dante, a comedy is basically a work written in a 'lowly' style (that is, in the vernacular) which has a happy ending.

From the *Decameron*

From the *Decameron, VI, 9*
Text: *Decameron*, edited by Cesare Segre, Mursia, 1987

You must know that in times past there were in our city many fine and praiseworthy customs, of which not one has lasted to our day, thanks to the avarice which, increasing in that city with the increase of riches, has driven them all out. One such custom was that in different parts of Florence well-born men of the districts got together and formed companies of a certain number, taking care to include only such as could stand the necessary expense, so that, today one of them, tomorrow another, and so on, all of them gave a banquet, each on his day, for the whole company. At those banquets they would often honour foreign notables, when any chanced to be there, and sometimes fellow-citizens. At least once a year they all dressed in the same way, and together they rode through the city on the most important anniversaries, and at times they managed arms, especially on the main feast days or when news of a victory or some other good fortune had reached the city.

Among those companies there was one which followed Messer Betto Brunelleschi. Betto and his friends had tried every way they could think of to get Guido Cavalcanti to join their company, and they had good reason for wanting him to. Apart from being one of the best logicians in the world and an excellent natural philosopher (things that band of friends cared little about), he was a very elegant and cultivated man and very fluent in his speech. Anything he wished to do, anything which befitted a gentleman, he could do better than anyone else. In addition to this, he was wealthy, and he really knew how to honour anyone he thought deserved it. However, Betto had never succeeded in persuading him to join them, and he and his friends thought that was because Guido was usually so lost in thought that he was oblivious to all around him. Incidentally, since he was influenced by the ideas of the Epicureans, the general belief was that his speculations were solely for the purpose of proving that God did not exist.

Now it happened one day that Guido came, as he often did, from Orsanmichele along the Corso degli Adimari to San Giovanni[1]. Those big marble tombs, which are now in Santa Reparata[2], were in those days still there around San Giovanni, with many others too, and he was by the porphyry columns there and those tombs and the door of San Giovanni, which was locked. Betto and his band came on horseback along the Piazza Santa Reparata and, seeing Guido there among the tombs, they said, 'Let's go and annoy him.' Spurring their horses in a mock attack, they were upon him before he was aware of them, and they said, 'Guido, you refuse to join our company; but just tell us something. When you have proved that God does not exist, what good will it do you?' Guido, seeing that he was hemmed in by them, answered immediately, 'You are the lords of this place, and may say what you like to me in your own home.' Then, laying his hand upon one of those big tombs, he leapt lightly over it and, extricating himself from them in this manner, went away.

They stared at each other, and said that he was a fool and that his reply did not mean anything, because they had no more to do with the place where they were than any other citizens, while Guido had no less to do with it than any of them. Then Betto turned to them and said, 'It is you who are fools. You fail to understand him. Politely and in a few words he has delivered the worst insult in the world. If you think about it, these tombs are the homes of the dead, because the dead are put there and stay there. When he says that they are our home he means that people like us are stupid illiterates in comparison with him and other learned men, that we are worse than dead men in fact, which is why when we are here we are at home.' And so all of them realised what Guido had meant, and they were ashamed of themselves. Never again did they annoy him, and they regarded Betto henceforth as an intelligent and subtle man.

NOTES

1. The Church of San Giovanni is now generally known as the Baptistery.
2. Santa Reparata is the church whose remains now lie under the Duomo, a few yards away from the Baptistery.

BIOGRAPHICAL NOTE

Giovanni Boccaccio was born in or near Florence in 1313, the son of a Florentine merchant. From around 1327 he settled in Naples, initially to study law, but becoming more and more involved in literature and literary studies, and it was here that he wrote his first works.

He returned to Florence in 1340 where he witnessed the atrocities of the 1348 Black Death – an event that was to be the inspiration for the *Decameron*, his most famous work. In 1350 he befriended Petrarch, and this relationship remained until Petrarch's death in 1374. It was around this time that he penned his *Life of Dante*, and began delivering a series of lectures on the *Divine Comedy*, despite the hostile reception they received from the Florentine authorities.

By the time of his death in 1375, Boccaccio had produced a number of other works including poems, allegories and romances. His writings have had a profound influence upon many English writers, with Chaucer, Shakespeare, Keats and Tennyson counting among his followers.

J.G. Nichols is a poet and translator. His published translations include the poems of Guido Gozzano (for which he was awarded the John Florio prize), Gabriele D'Annunzio, Giacomo Leopardi, and Petrarch (for which he won the Monselice Prize).

HESPERUS PRESS – 100 PAGES

Hesperus Press, as suggested by the Latin motto, is committed to bringing near what is far – far both in space and time. Works written by the greatest authors, and unjustly neglected or simply little known in the English-speaking world, are made accessible through new translations and a completely fresh editorial approach. Through these short classic works, each little more than 100 pages in length, the reader will be introduced to the greatest writers from all times and all cultures.

For more information on Hesperus Press, please visit our website: **www.hesperuspress.com**

To place an order, please contact:
Grantham Book Services
Isaac Newton Way
Alma Park Industrial Estate
Grantham
Lincolnshire NG31 9SD
Tel: +44 (0) 1476 541080
Fax: +44 (0) 1476 541061
Email: orders@gbs.tbs-ltd.co.uk

SELECTED TITLES FROM HESPERUS PRESS

Gustave Flaubert *Memoirs of a Madman*
Alexander Pope *Scriblerus*
Ugo Foscolo *Last Letters of Jacopo Ortis*
Anton Chekhov *The Story of a Nobody*
Joseph von Eichendorff *Life of a Good-for-nothing*
Mark Twain *The Diary of Adam and Eve*
Victor Hugo *The Last Day of a Condemned Man*
Joseph Conrad *Heart of Darkness*
Edgar Allan Poe *Eureka*
Emile Zola *For a Night of Love*
Daniel Defoe *The King of Pirates*
Giacomo Leopardi *Thoughts*
Nikolai Gogol *The Squabble*
Franz Kafka *Metamorphosis*
Herman Melville *The Enchanted Isles*
Leonardo da Vinci *Prophecies*
Charles Baudelaire *On Wine and Hashish*
William Makepeace Thackeray *Rebecca and Rowena*
Wilkie Collins *Who Killed Zebedee?*
Théophile Gautier *The Jinx*
Charles Dickens *The Haunted House*
Luigi Pirandello *Loveless Love*
Fyodor Dostoevsky *Poor People*
E.T.A. Hoffmann *Mademoiselle de Scudéri*
Henry James *In the Cage*
Francesco Petrarch *My Secret Book*
D.H. Lawrence *The Fox*
Percy Bysshe Shelley *Zastrozzi*